The Bible of Ngo Cho Kun

Chinese Gentle Art Complete

Tiong Hua Yu Sut Tai Tsuan

中華柔術大全

DISCLAIMER

The author and publisher of this book are NOT RESPONSIBLE in any manner whatsoever for any injury that may result from practicing the techniques and/or following the instructions given within. Since the physical activities described herein may be too strenuous in nature for some readers to engage in safely, it is essential that a physician be consulted prior to training.

First Published April 14, 2014 by Tambuli Media

ISBN: 978-0692205419

Cover Design and Interior Graphics by Tyler Rea
https://www.linkedin.com/pub/tyler-rea/31/337/6a

Original Sketches by Robert Cory Del Medico
http://www.advancefamilychiroandmassage.ca/

Mark Wiley, Alexander Co, Russ Smith
Beng Kiam Athletic Association
Makati City, Philippines, 2013

Chinese Gentle Art Complete

Tiong Hua Yu Sut Tai Tsuan

Written in 1917 by
Yu Chiok Sam

English Translation, 2009 & 2013 by
Alexander Lim Co

Additonal Translation by
Russ L. Smith

Edited by
Mark V. Wiley

With the Support of

Philippine Beng Kiam Athletic Association
American Beng Hong Athletic Association

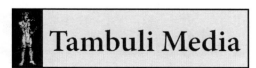

Tambuli Media

Spring House, PA (USA)
www.TambuliMedia.com

Chua Giok Beng (1853 - 1910)
Founder of Ngo Cho Kun

FOREWORD

Grandmaster Benito Tan

April 02, 2014
Philippine Beng Kiam Athletic Association
Binondo, Manila, Philippines

I am pleased to announce the publication of *Tiong Hua Yu Sut Tai Tsuan,* translated differently as "Complete Way of the Chinese Gentle Art," or more simply as "*Chinese Gentle Art Complete*," for its composition as a comprehensive book on the techniques, drills and forms of our feared Ngo Cho Kun fighting art. No matter how you translate the title, this book will always be referred to as "The Bible of Ngo Cho," for it is the first known publication on our art, is little understood, and holds within it many secrets.

My father, Tan Ka Hong, was a student of my grandfather, Tan Kiong Beng, who himself was one of the 10 disciples of the art's founder, Sijo Chua Giok Beng. The author of this book, Yu Chiok Sam, was a classmate of my grandfather and a co-disciple of Sijo Chua. Although my grandfather and Mr. Yu both learned from Chua, the way the art has been handed down is somewhat different among them, and indeed is different among all of the groups of the founder's 10 disciples, known as the "Ngo Cho Ten Tigers." Within our specific Beng Kiam lineage, we maintain 44 basic empty-hand sets, plus more advanced ones, two-person sets and many not even mentioned within this book. What's more, some of the technique descriptions do not match our way of doing them. Many of the forms described in this book also do not correspond exactly as they have been passed in our line. But then, kung-fu is not precise, it is an individual expression and evolves, not to mention that not all students pay attention in class or can recall precisely their master's teachings!

Well, differences aside, I congratulate Sifu Alex Co for translating this rare and important book and for publishing it with his American disciple, Mark Wiley. And of course we are also indebted to Dr. Wiley's top student, Russ Smith, for his great help. You have brought the past to the present so that we may understand the richness of this art more fully and completely.

1st TRANSLATOR'S PREFACE

Alexander Lim Co

December 15, 2013
Philippine Beng Kiam Athletic Association
Makati Branch, Metro Manila, Philippines

Chinese Gentle Art Complete was published by Yu Chiok Sam, alias Yu Hong Piao, in 1917. Yu was one of the "Ngo Cho Ten Tigers," the top 10 disciples of Chua Giok beng, the founder of Ngo Cho Kun or Five Ancestor Fist Kung-Fu. Yu intended his book to be used as an instructional manual for school students in China. Yu authored two more books, one intended for instructors, and another one for use in the field of medicine. Unfortunately, the printing press handling the publication of these works was bombed and burned during the Sino-Japanese War. Only the first volume was printed, with limited copies in circulation and highly treasured by Ngo Cho Kun instructors. The intention of Yu in writing these books on Ngo Cho Kun was principally to clear the confusion among the art's instructors. The confusion was generally created because of the founder's teaching method, which was based on the individual student's physical attributes and physique. Chua Giok Beng also taught slight variations of the Ngo Cho Kun forms in different localities. There seemed to be no standard, and so ***Chinese Gentle Art Complete*** became the authority to define the essence of the Ngo Cho Kun system.

The few who were able to get copies of this book viewed them as sacred property, keeping its contents to themselves. The book was so secretive that only favored disciples were able to access it, through the trust and confidence of the masters. Many considered and referred to it as the ***Ngo Cho Bible***.

During the process of writing this book, my sigong, Tan Kiong Beng, was invited by the founder himself, Chua Giok Beng, to the home of Yu Chiok Sam. It was in Yu's home that Tan and Chua reviewed a copy of the draft manuscript. Tan Kiong Beng is also one of the "Ngo Cho TenTigers" and at this time was given a copy of the contents of the book. My Sifu, Tan Ka Hong (Tan Kiong Beng's son), further expanded the book and retitled it, ***Ngo Cho Kun Complete***. Yu's original book had no listing of the two-man forms

or remainder of the 44 solo forms. I was one of the fortunate few allowed to read Tan's book, which was kept from the student group and only shared among in-door disciples. This book remains secretive to this day.

In the early 1980s, my sihing, Alfonzo Ang Hua Kun, went to China and was able to get a photocopy of the original *Chinese Gentle Art Complete*. He gave me a copy and made me swear to its secrecy. My sihing has long since passed away and I have forever treasured this book.

In 1998, I entrusted my student Mark V. Wiley with a rough English translation of this original book and helped him form the American Beng Hong Athletic Association. A dacade later, in 2009, in recognition of his discipline and ernest efforts to promote the Ngo Cho style, and my trust in him, I gave Mark a copy of my personal, original copy.

In 2008, Lions' Press of Taiwan reprinted *Chinese Gentle Art Complete* (in Chinese) for mass distribution, but the book has little use for non practitioners, and likewise for Ngo Cho Kun practitioners who have little knowledge of the true essence of the art. The book consists only of names and postures with no photos or visuals, making it hard to understand both by practitioners and non-practitioners alike.

Mark V. Wiley and his top student, Russ Smith, have collaborated to improve on my rough English translations and they asked me have the final check on all postures and pictures, so the contents of this book can easily be understood and interpreted by both practitioners and non-practitioners. Although it is impossible to pose for everything written on the book, we have decided to show the basic postures amd techniques, some preparatory exercises and solo forms. In the future, we will come out with a separate volume with full illustrations of the 38 forms contained here.

The interpretation of Ngo Cho Kun material presented herein is based on the perspective of my sigong, Tan Kiong Beng, a direct disciple of founder Chua Giok Beng (Cai Yu Ming, in Mandarin). His teachings were transmitted to me through my sifu, Tan Ka Hong, through the Philippine Beng Kiam Athletic Association.

I can honestly say as a martial artist and with my wide exposure in the field of martial arts, that this book is by far the best in terms of authenticity when it comes to the Ngo Cho Kun style of kung-fu. If we can entice martial arts practitioners to get into this style, given its true essence, then our efforts for publishing this book shall not be in vain.

2nd TRANSLATOR'S PREFACE

Russ L. Smith

March 17, 2014
American Beng Hong Athletic Association
Zephyrhills, Florida, USA

I am very excited to write this forward for this turn of the century book on the Fukian martial art of Ngo Cho Kun. As a long-time practitioner of Okinawan Goju-ryu, I became interested in the historical roots of, and potential influences on, the transmission of martial arts from southern China (Fuzhou in particular) to the small island of Okinawa, Japan.

Eventually, I was fortunate to make acquaintance with Dr. Mark Wiley in preparation for the development of a research and distribution effort on southern Chinese martial arts. Knowing that he not only practiced but taught Ngo Cho Kun, and learned from none other than the famous Sifu Alexander Lim Co, I began making arrangements to meet and train with him in person. To this day I remain a student of Dr. Wiley and have become an Officer of the American Beng Hong Athletic Association.

As my training continued, Sifu Wiley began to share with me what had traditionally been rare information, typically passed down from sifu to todai; information largely from a book, colloquially known as the "Bible of Ngo Cho Kun," indicating the place of honor this information held in the hearts of the past practitioners of the art. The information, containing principles, techniques, training drills, empty-hand and weapons forms was partly translated by Sigong Co and provided to his trusted student, Sifu Wiley. The portion passed down to me served as a "Rosetta Stone" of sorts, allowing me to read and understand the remainder of the document and (later) help with many of the simpler, technical aspects of the translation.

Today, Ngo Cho Kun is amidst a revival in the East, primarily due to its installment as *the* martial art of the Southern Shaolin Temple in Quanzhou, China. Because of this resurgence, the turn of the century technical manual, ***Chinese Gentle Art Complete***, was re-released in Chinese. As a result of this public unveiling, I was able to convince Sifu Wiley and, with his assistance, Sigong Co, of the value of releasing to the world a full English translation. It is my pleasure to be a part of this important project that brings a century's old Ngo Cho Kun manual to the Western world. I am also proud that through the efforts of both my Sifu and Sigong, the book's missing pictures have been added.

EDITOR'S PREFACE

Dr. Mark V. Wiley

January 07, 2014
American Beng Hong Athletic Association
Philadelphia, Pennsylvania USA

We have translated and published, for the first time in English and with photographs, this antique book on Fukien kung-fu. It is the oldest known book on the Five Ancestor Fist style known as Ngo Cho Kun and Wu Chu Chuan, and has been out of print for a century! It was written in an old Hokkien dialect, which is not well known today. These points have made this book treasured by the few who possess a copy, and difficult for many to understand.

Interestingly, while the topic is specifically Ngo Cho Kun, author Yu Chiok Sam refers to the style as "Chinese Gentle Art" (*Tiong Hua Yu Sut*), although it is referred to by name in the original Prefaces. And the most important form (*Sam Chien*, "Three Battles") and the art's main stance (*chien be*) are also not referred to herein by their standard names.

Moreover, either the author or the printer had an odd way of arranging content within the book. Chapters on basics are inserted between chapters on advanced forms. An odd method of numbering the material was used; some of which are techniques, others applications or exercises, and then the numbers just stop. Also strange, there are two distinct sections on the "Opening Method" and "Closing Method," a full 10 pages apart. Logically, these would go together. And the single and double long and short hand techniques would also be grouped accordingly.

With this in mind, we have reorganized the author's material and chapters into a more clear format. Editorially, when we have had to make notes to the reader, we have done so in italics, with the words *Editor's Note* preceding them. And while we have done our best to include as many photographs as possible, with so much material it was impossible to include photos for every movement. This, coupled with the fact that Chinese does not use prepositions and verb forms, has made translation and presentation difficult. But well worth it!

We hope you enjoy this first-ever illustrated and bi-lingual Chinese/English edition of **Chinese Gentle Art Complete**, considered by many practitioners as "The Bible of Ngo Cho Kun." If you are looking for a teacher, resources are in the Appendix.

TABLE OF CONTENTS
目次

VOLUME 1

Fundamentals

VOLUME 2

Gentle Art Training Methods

VOLUME 3

Standard Practice Methods

VOLUME 4

Impromptu Movement Methods

VOLUME 5

National Techniques, Six Arts Methods

CHINESE GENTLE ART COMPLETE – PREFACE
中華柔術大全 序

神州積弱。殆及百年。識時之彥。謂非振興體育。興德智兩育並重 。則不足以反弱為強。顧體育亦多術矣。今學校之所教。社會之所尚。所謂德日瑞典。諸種體育之常識。已漸形普及。何獨於中國固有之拳術。研究者乃絕尠其人。夫拳術國技也。亦國粹也。遠觀戚南塘紀效新書。近觀日俄戰爭紀要。而知其效用至大。宜於古而未嘗不利今。故中國不欲振興則已。中國而欲振興體育。甯能遺棄拳術而弗研究邪。鄙人家學淵源。治拳術二十餘年。曩囿於風氣秘塞。未敢出所學授人。以震駭世俗。而於國之粹之論失弗傳。又私用杞憂。勢不能終秘所學而弗以授人。今承各界慈惠組織斯書。拳術復興。今豈其時乎。鄙人亦惟於向學者之多寡。興各界贊成者之熱誠興否卜之耳。

中華民國六年秋月晉江尤鳳標祝三誌於泉州國技傳習所

China had long been known as a feeble nation for a century. The scholars with foresight had clearly declared that the only way to revive our country from the frail to the powerful was to empower both the physical education and the moral and intellectual education of the Chinese people. There were multiple types of sport, such as those that were introduced from Germany, Japan and Switzerland, and those that were taught at schools and those that were prevailing in the society, had been popularized gradually. However, why had the Chinese native sports (martial arts) been studied by no one? Chinese martial arts, the national sports, were the essence of the national culture. The early record of martial arts could be found in the *Qi Nan Tang Ji Xiao Xin* book, and can be found as late as in the *Memorandum of War of Japan and Russia*. The records all suggested the greatness and efficiency of martial arts in the practice of wars. They were feasible to both the ancient war and the modern war. Therefore, as long as the Chinese society needed to promote sport, then the martial arts would not be ignored. My family had a history of 20 years in practicing martial arts. Limited to the tradition of my family, I was not allowed to show and teach my martial arts to non family members, otherwise I might go against the established customs of society. However, the maintenance and conveyance of martial arts led them to begin disappearing gradually and my overwhelming concerns about the situation of martial arts made me disclose my skills to the public for learning and recording. Hereto, I was encouraged by all the societies to compose this book for the public, in order to meet the opportunity of a revival of martial arts sports. I could only pray the numbers of learners and the passion of the public toward the national martial arts skills will follow.

In the autumn of the Zhonghua Minguo VI,
at the Resident of Jin Jiang You Feng Biao, byYu Hong Piao
The Gentle Art Institute of Quanzhou, Fujian Province

拳術一道，純用武力，不曰剛而曰柔，者何哉。蓋則恐易傷人，而柔善為衛己，術固不可濫施也。或曰精斯者，世鮮敵手，正好爭雄於環球之界。然已擒虎斬蛟龍之猛，用以對壘沖鋒，其以槍炮之攻堅及遠何。且擅機器以威天下者，有火艇之飛空，鐵之潛海艦。均非可以吾術之柔克也。柔術之利，在以近距而不在以用遠，兵可接則近之，寇可獲之則追之。能制人而不為人指，且可以自固，而預備不虞，是焉不得亟講也。尤君祝三刀弓之技，秉承家傳。弱冠之年領袖武攜，其韜略可知己，乃若拳棒切磨則師資蔡氏，而特造宏深。以是術奮於戰場，何難拔幟而樹幟，以是術傳之藝圃，且得育才而成才。夫柔術之學有傳人，少傳書，君有心名世，獨出機軸，組織成編，其中奇正相生，無數法門。從難方諸孫武十三篇，武侯八陣圖，亦足資保障敵愾之實益。習體操者以是為宗旨，則國造士之得力在斯焉。而是書之立言，千古不朽已，是為序。

中華民國三年瑞月南安蓮塘楊鼎豫

Martial arts were the way to improve strength, so its training was hard and rigid, so why was it called "gentle art?" Because Five Ancestor Boxing was so strong that it might hurt people, only soft application of it in self-defense could prevent it from being applied abusively. Someone might misunderstand that if the practitioners were so good at it that they might be the leaders of a world without enemies. However, the capability of Ngo Cho Boxing in arresting tigers and killing dragons were actually useless in facing to the power of long distance weapons (i.e., guns and canons.) Among the best weapons of the world, the power of the rocket could go miles high to the sky and the power of the submarine could be down miles deep in the oceans. However, the power of martial arts is not comparable to any of them. The power of martial arts was best at short distance, not at long distance. It could be effective in wrestling, in the situation that short weapons are used, where the enemy could be caught, then the power of martial arts was best. It was also the best in self-defense. Mr. Yu Chiok Sam mastered the archery and horsemanship of his family tradition. When he was 20 years old, he was the best warrior amongst his peers so his present experiences and skills were great. The skills of unarmed and armed martial arts of Mr. Yu were taught by Mr. Chua, and so these skills were even more profound. If one could master these skills they could easily win in combats and battles. If the skills were taught at educational institutes, the trainees would be able to be the best and became the descendents of the martial arts. However, the martial arts usually were transferred in person and not published in a book. Mr. Yu preferred to transfer his skills in a different way: he published his skills in a book. Among these skills, it contains many methods, techniques, and so on. Including military army array, such as Sunbin Thirteen Chapters, Wuhou Eight Diagrams, which were sufficient to protect for the benefit of a country. People who practice these skills will build up the power of our country. Therefore, the contents of this book would last thousands of years, and therefore I made this preface for congratulation.

In the Spring of the Third Year of China Minguo
At Nanan Liantang by Yang Tah Siong

夫拳術一端，古今名流輩出，世所見者，五祖拳棒耳。第年湮代遠，遺傳失真，以致學者紛如，無從窺秘。即略知門徑，有多好勇鬥狠，勇以私而卻以公。此士大夫所以羞稱，而肆業者少也。吾夫子蔡玉明，曩以弓馬游泮，兼通五祖拳法：白鶴手、齊天指、太祖足、達尊身、羅漢步。予親受業，見夫步武得式，矯如龍鳳，散若沉魚。心誠求之垂二十余載。竊思古今拳藝，歷久而失本來，緣口傳無圖書可考耳。不揣固陋，以吾夫子所授，並家傳秘術，參考維新教授圖法篡為一編，如體操之有秩序，以便軍國民之操習。第恐掛以漏萬，未敢出而問世。今歲任泉州中學、佩實高等小學國技教員，值運動會，頗為各界歡迎，省視學鄭、道視學江獎籍有加。又見是編，蒙二先生許可之，且曰"使我國尚武精神於焉大振，其在茲乎"，促付剞劂以公同好，該校諸教員復極力贊同，用敢以一得之愚貢諸同胞，高明君子其我諒乎！綜之業斯藝者，要使泰山崩於前而色不變，麋鹿興於左而目不瞬，而尤注重道德，毋以強悍自恃，而滿眼空盡歐亞。誠如是，則柔術思過半矣。

中華民國四年冬月晉江尤祝三誌於泉州佩實中學

As far as performers of martial arts, there were so many famous masters from ancient time to the present time. What we admired most was Five Ancestor Boxing and staff, which was created a long time ago. Many parts have been lost and missed though learners who were ardent, but no one could make the best application. Even those who knew a little, were strict in keeping it for their own benefit and unwilling to share the benefit of what they learned. It was the noble people who were training it and few people could develop the skills completely. My teacher Chua Giok Beng had been good at both archery and horsemanship and thus enrolled in the higher education institute for many years. He also had been proficient in Ngo Cho Kun such as: crane hand, monkey finger, Grand Emperor foot, Da Mo body, and lohan step. I had been receiving his instruction personally, and witnessed his marvelous step skills, supple and flexible body movements. I had practiced it about 20 years. I personally believed that the Ngo Cho Boxing developed through many years and has lost its original versions because it was transferred via individual's words, not recorded in books. I thus began to compile what I was taught by my teacher and by my family with reference of illustration methods to gather into a book manuscript. It was arranged similar to the gymnastic methods so that it was easier to be practiced by military and non-military. I used to worry that it might not be perfect and did not publish it for the public. This year, when I was the martial arts teacher of the Quanzhou Middle School and the Peishi Higher Elementary School, the martial arts performance of my students was awarded by Province and County Department of Education in the athletic contest; and the martial art book manuscript that I compiled was reviewed by the officers of the Department of Education, and received encouragement again. With the permissions of the Department of Education, "it aims to promote our spirit of physical education if we can publish the book and its significance will be great." Thus, in a short period of time, I put it into publication to share it with peers and the publication was encouraged by my colleagues as well. If there were any errors, please allow time to make corrections. The main goal of Ngo Cho Kun requires that no change to the prctitioner can be seen even if the Tai Mountain corrupts ahead, and his eyes do not divert from his opponent even if deer are jumping and hopping to his side; it emphasizes the ethics such that no one can impose their ill will or hold the world as their servant. If this does not happen, the self-development learned through practice of the Chinese Gentle Art is only half-way achieved.

In Winter of Fourth year of China Minguo
By Yu Chiok Sam at QuanZhou Pei Shi Middle School

柔術一書，世所罕見。歷史中雖備載英豪，然徒言狀貌武功，而少專書圖式，間有余法可考者，亦不過雜錦零霞，出自私家手跡，東鱗西爪，見於說部舊傳，皆無完全之足徵也。吾友尤君祝三少功詩書，長學弓馬，弱冠才逾，武科獨佔。其后好游藝圃，切磋卅年之功，遍訪名家，搜羅五祖之術，聚精會神拾遺補闕。恐秘傳之忘佚，遂草創而成書。早擬刊本問世，屢因事中輟。今學滄海橫流，外侮時亟，尚武精神，尤為急務。秉國鈞者，切切以拳術一門施諸學界。然部令甫頒，尤君即受桐城學校之聘矣，課余假日酌古准今，爰將舊制別入新式，標題分類，圖明法賅，大綱以體操為用，柔術為體，相機度勢，即體用之兼賅，應手得心，尤剛柔以相濟，便於學子演操，宜以教員指授，誠今之武經也，又奚佚拔山超海，暴虎伐蛟龍，始稱妙法也哉。

中華民國四年南安呂春榮紫瓊序於官橋學校

A book on Chinese gentle art was rarely seen in the world. Throughout history, though books recorded many heroes and masters of Chinese gentle art, their appearances, statures and achievements were all recorded well, few books recorded illustrations on the martial arts skills. Even though there were some books containing skills of martial arts, they were either small pieces, or scattered in with other contents and they can not be used for practice. My friend, Yu Chiok Sam, was skilled in poetry and literature in childhood and was excellent in archery, horsemanship in his elder age. At the age of 20 years, he had been the best in poetry and literature, and his martial arts skills were even much better. Afterward, at 30 years, he visited many places and met many masters in communicating martial arts, in order to collect, polish and complete the Ngo Cho Boxing skills. To prevent the collections of Ngo Cho skills from becoming lost, he compiled these into a book manuscript. Initially, his publication plan was delayed for some reasons. Now, the society and county is in a high risk of invasion by foreign countries, thus the spirit of promotion of martial art is important, urgent and necessary. The statutes and rules also had been promoting martial arts as content taught in the education institutes. When the rules were issued, Mr. Yu just received an offer to be the teacher at the Tongcheng School. During his spare time from teaching, Mr. Yu compiled his skills, incorporating them with a new illustration format for this book. It contained the titles on each category, and showed clear illustrations with brief instructions on it. It was followed with rules of gymnastics and incorporated the content of the Chinese gentle art, which benefited both of the advantages of the two skills, thus it would be easier to learn by students and easier to teach by teachers. It was really the present "Bible of the Martial Arts" because it would enable performers with ability to move mountains, surpass seas, fight tigers and defeat dragons. It was a true marvelous skill!

In the Fourth year of China Minguo
At Naan Lu Chun Guanqiao School By Yeng Tzi Wan

中國拳術。濫觴於蚩尤之以角觝人。於是有角觝之戲。有搏刀勾卒擲塗賭跳之法。應
劭漢書武帝本紀注。角者角技也。觝者相觝觸也。文穎曰。兩兩相當。角力角技藝射
御也。韓昌黎曹成王碑。王親教之。搏力勾卒嬴越之法。原註嬴秦也。商子農戰篇。
有搏民力以待外事。則搏力者秦法也。在傳越王為左右勾卒。杜為勾伍相錯。別為
左右屯。則勾卒者越法也。運鑑齊記。齊王昭業興左右微服走市里。好於世祖崇陽陵
隊中。擲塗賭跳。作諸鄙戲。使臣因識齊王好拳勇。然則中古以前之拳術如是而已。
中古以后。宋太祖。少林僧。張三豐。張鬆溪。始以拳術著名。法秘技精。常能張空
拳擊賊累十百。雖操利刃遇之無或幸免。拳術進步於茲可徵。而內外家之分。亦即起
於時。大抵外家祖少林。法主於搏人。然跳踉奮耀。或失之疏。而見乘於敵。內家祖
鬆溪。法主御侮非遇困厄不輕法。發之當者立靡。無隙可乘。故內家之術尤善。而自
戚南塘紀效新書出世。謂刀槍劍鉤鐮之類。莫不先由拳術活動身手。於是拳術之效用
愈大。習武備者弗能偏廢。請世營制未發。教練卒興拳法相出人。兼精拳術者則以驍
勇善戰稱。近則東鄰得其諸余。用諸短兵相接。而大收其效，於旅順戰爭者矣。嗟乎
中國士大夫毋因時事變易，芻狗拳術，謂不足以自強而強國也，抑毋謂習拳術者，盡
於出草澤不逞之徒，而非軍人學習，普通國民所應肄業也，吾友尤君祝三，治拳術近
二十年，精深可知，顧能不吝所學，出其秘藏以公諸世，可謂有心人。別有懷抱，吾
年未三十，自顧心力氣體，已無復之雄邁、堅強矯健、便捷。傳青主不雲乎。咕嗶能
壞人筋骨。吾以自懼，行且從尤君，研究斯術以藥吾病，並蘄他日見諸實用。無負此
身。尤君其許我否乎。是為敘。

中華民國五年五月溫陵李濃序泉州中學校

It had been said that Chinese martial arts originated from the legend of Chi Yu who fought against people with the horn (jiao), which developed into martial arts skills of wrestling, combat skills such as weapon fight (bo dao), military array (gou zu), casting (zhi tu), high jumping (du tiao), etc. According to the record of the *Han Book - Chapter Wu Emperor's Biography*, "jiao" means the wrestling skills; "di" (against) means to fight. Wen Ying noted: two persons to combat each other with wrestling, skills of archery and slingshot, etc. According to *Hang Chang Li and Cao Cheng Emperor Steel*, the emperor taught the wrestling skills et cetera in person. In the *Sang Zi - Chapter Agriculture and Fight*, it was reported to train people in wrestling for defense against enemy. So wrestling is derived from Qin's skill. It was said that Yue Emperor performed military array, the army advanced in the form of rectangle shape linked together to defend and with other armies settled at the two sides of the main army. So military array skill is derived from Yue's army skill. In the report of *Comprehensive Mirror to Aid in Government - Chapter Qi*, Emperor Qi Zhao Ye, and his companies, changed into ordinary cloths and walked in the towns. He used to contesting the casting, high jumping and other skill games with them at the Shi Zu Chingyang Tomb. Visitors therefore knew Emperor Qi was good in wrestling; it is the record of the martial arts skills before the Song Dynasty. Since the Song Dynasty, Song Tai Chu, monks of Shaolin Temple, Chang San Feng, Chang Song Shi, are all famous in their martial arts. Their practices are confidential; the skills yet are superb: they can defeat dozens of unarmed thieves, thieves with arms could not avoid being defeated. The great progress of martial arts can be seen. The discrepancies of internal style and external style also originated at that time. Generally, external styles originated from the Shaolin Temple, the techniques focused on attacking, yet the skills of jumping, leaping, hopping and climbing were not perfect and therefore left chances for enemies. The internal styles originated from Chang Song Xi, its techniques on defense and application can only be used endangered. The skills could kill any enemies immediately and there was no chance for the enemy to fight back. Therefore, the internal style is especially better. Since the publication of Qin Nan Tang's book, *Ji Xiao Xin Shu*, all the weapon-based skills were based upon the excise of wrestling skills, etc. Therefore, the significance of wrestling skills, etc. were greater, and the practices of martial arts could not ignore both wrestling skills and weapons skills. In the army, solders were taught martial arts. Those who were good at combat also were good in martial arts. The recent battle with Japan, Lu Shun Battle, was mainly a close fight with short arms, and the effect was significant. Unfortunately, Chinese officers and scholars degraded martial arts, that they were not sufficient to empower our people and our country, or since martial arts practitioners were all low-class people, so they should not be learned by army and citizens due to the changing situation. My friend, Yu Chiok Sam, practiced martial arts for almost 20 years. One can only imagine how experienced and profound his skills were. He could open up what he learned and publish his confidential techniques for the public. His contribution was so meaningful and unselfish. When I was younger than 30 years old, I used to feel that my physical capability was no longer strong, skillful and flexible. It is said that some of my habits could damage bones and tendons. So I was aware of it and sought out Mr. Yu to learn martial arts, in order to cure my symptoms and to use them it for self-defense applications. I am thankful for my experience with martial arts and Mr. Yu therefore allowed me to write of it in this preface.

In May of Fifth year of China Minguo
at Wenling Linongxue Quan Zhou Middle School by Lee Long

今之世界，萬國角雄之世界也。凡有血氣者，孰奮發尚武精神，挽祖國之衰弱，爭長雄以全球。故體操拳藝，誠今天所不可缺諸。尤君鳳標，別字祝三，夙承庭訓，以弓馬入泮。有念及斯，熱心拳術，遍游藝圃，廣閱教師，親授以蔡君玉鳴，盡心力為普通五技，爰思夫五祖去此雲遙，妙法真傳雖在，然無書可考，無圖可徵，恐時代滄桑，流而日下，不免遺真。於是殫半身之精力，究斯藝最真妙，於體操相貫通，輯成是編，付梓問世。從茲以往，方針既定，目的變通，不特使我同胞操習者有標准，后之操習者有規范，將見英氣勃勃，雄風決決，國勢日張，駕歐亞而直上。

中華民國二年冬月南安楊年華序於蓮塘學校

In oru present time, all countries fought for the leadership of the world. No other person had the guts to work harder and harder in promoting the spirit of the martial arts, in order to save the poor situation of the country and to boost the country to the top of the world. Therefore, the gymnastics martial arts are so indispensible in the current society. Mr. Yu Chiok Sam, alias Zhusan, was born into a family with traditions in practicing archery and horsemanship and he was accepted into the higher education institute for his expertise. Under such a circumstance, he was keen on martial arts. He has visited many schools, discussed with many masters of martial arts and received instructions from Mr. Chua Giok Beng. Mr. Yu tried his best and devoted himself to the practice of Ngo Cho Kun skills. However, he used to worry that the founding of Ngo Cho Boxing had happened a long time ago, though the true version of the skills existed, there was no book for learners to turn to, no illustrations for performer to look at. In order to avoid the loss of the true record, he therefore devoted his life efforts in compiling the most essential part of Ngo Cho Kun, incorporating it with the gymnastics and compiled them into this book for publication. From now on, the aims of Ngo Cho Boxing were made; the goal of Ngo Cho Kun was built. The book not only set up the standard of practitioners, but also the rules of the practitioners. It would be expected soon that our people should be strapping, brawny and the reputation of our country would rise day by day so that it would rise up and surpass all the other countries in Europe and Asia.

In the Winter of the 2nd Year of China Minguo
At Naan Lian Tang School by Yu Lian Ho

INTRODUCTORY REMARKS
例言

一。此書專為體育上。全部之運動。是學者有尚武精神。故名之曰。中華柔術大全。一。古人所授拳術。皆尚口傳。況世遠年湮。歧流雜出。學者無從窺秘。得本書而研究之。思過半矣。一。衛生家注重體育。今以秘傳之拳術。參究新法。俾與體操。互相發明。凡以應社會之要求也。一。運動以少時漸進。得其姿勢於體育上。不無少補。加練習太猛進殊與衛生有妨碍。學者慎之。一。全書分為五編。由淺而深。隨機操習。易於領悟。以期進步之敏捷。一。第一編述運用之目的。而姿勢並開始。完全。順步、及足步、雙單手長短機一百十四法。機手同類者附之，兼體操口令。以便公共練習。一。第二編述演習法。五章四十二節。便以初運動。以應高等小學用。一。第三編述操練法三十八套。有剛有柔。以應中學、軍隊、及專門體育之用。一。第四編述臨時法八段。分為四十八節。以應運動會之選用也。一。第五編述國技六藝法即槍、刀、劍、戟、鐵鞭、棍、以應專門體育之用。一。動作之姿勢。撮附照相精法九十九圖。其與上冊第一編參照閱之。編者識

Lion Dance, Beng Kiam Athletic Association, Manila, Philippines 1950s

This book is specifically intended as a manual for a complete program of physical exercise with the aim of promoting martial arts spirit. Hence, the name *Chinese Gentle Art Complete*. In ancient times, martial arts were taught and handed down through oral transmission and through the passage of time the art became diluted and confusing, making it difficult for the students to understand, more so its secrets. If you have this book and learn through it, it can assist you in accomplishing your goals.

Athletes emphasize exercise, and by using these once secretive martial arts and combining them with modern methods of physical exercise, these can be adapted by the general public's desire for an overall physical exercise program. While exercising, we tend to progress gradually, so by using the postures as an exercise, we must likewise progress gradually according to our ability in order to maintain good health. This is a reminder of what beginners should be aware of.

The book is divided into five volumes progressing from simple to advanced exercises, which makes it easy to understand so you can progress quickly.

The first volume explains the objective of this exercise. It contains the beginning and complete postures of the steps, footworks and the 114 single and double, long and short techniques. The techniques that are similar are grouped together with accompanying command drills to facilitate for large group practices.

The second volume explains the training methods which are divided into five chapters and 42 sections. This is suited as an introductory exercise program for elementary and high school levels.

The third volume explains the practice of 38 forms. There are rigid ones as well as gentle forms, which are suited for high school, military and physical instructors.

The fourth volume explains the eight chapters of extracted, simplified methods which are further subdivided into 48 sections. These are specifically to be used by athletic gyms and associations.

The fifth volume explains the six arts of martial arts weaponry, which are the spear, broadsword, short sword, halberd, iron ruler and staff, to be used for physical exercises.

The postures are supplemented by 99 pictures which can be used as training aids for chapter one. (***Editor's Note:*** *The original book printing did not inculude these pictures. For this edition, we have included roughly 725 pictures to illustrate the written material.*)

—*The Author/Editor*

Grandmaster Benito Tan Poses in Hong Be Tsai

Volume 1

第一編

FUNDAMENTALS

<table>
<tr><td>

1

</td><td>

THE PURPOSE OF THE GENTLE ART
柔術之目的

</td></tr>
</table>

Anfonzo Ang Hua Kun

二十世紀，一武裝和平時代也。文明愈進步，殺人之器，亦講求愈精。而柔術一門，逐若天演淘汰之列，不知槍湮彈雨，賁育原無所施，而短兵相接時則柔術尚矣。日俄一役，其彰明較著者也，且流水不腐,戶樞不蠹。研究衛生學者，大多以運動為增進身體之健康，夫運動法日術相接之佳良，又熟有過柔術者乎。吾國滿清未造，積弱相仍，摺紳士夫，縛雞無力。光復以 後,當軸者稍知文弱之不足競存也，於是學校兼課柔術之文，然則柔術雖一技之微，而小足以保身，大足以強種，使上行下效，化病夫為健兒，中國前途庶有生氣乎。

The 20th century is a time of war and peace. The advancement of science has improved the weapons of war to a very advanced stage. With the use of guns and bullets, the rigorous training of hand-to-hand combat has almost been eliminated. But when infantry confront each other, the arts of empty hand combat, or martial arts, are still excellent tools. Their practical applications were evident during the Sino-Japanese-Russian war. Running water doesn't stagnate, and a constantly used door hinge doesn't rust. Most hygienists agree that exercise helps develop a strong, healthy body. But, can the benefits of Western physical exercise be better than kung-fu?

During the post-Manchu era, people still pursued a scholarly education. But the scholars were all weak in physique. But after the Republic, the leaders of the nation realized the insufficiency of promoting only education and neglecting the exercise of the physique. That is why kung-fu is now a supplemental subject in schools. Although kung-fu is just a small factor in the development of the people, it can help in developing the individual and in turn produce a healthy, strong population. People in all levels can become healthy individuals, rather than the former "sick men of Asia." In this way, there will be a greater future for China.

2

GENTLE ART APPLICATION

柔術之應用

Alfonzo Ang Hua Kun & Alex Co

人身兩手足而已，然善運用者則通身皆手眼矣。習柔術者，平居手舞足蹈習與性成，大敵在前，無不以一當十，縱橫跳躍，不可捉摸，此其故何，知運用之法，約為四端。

A man has only two hands and two feet. To be able to use them effectively, the eyes and the hands should be coordinated. A trained kung-fu practitioner can move his hands and feet gracefully, as though he were dancing. Once he masters this art, he can defend himself easily when confronted with an opponent. He can still manage even against 10 opponents, due to his dexterity in moving and jumping around. His opponent cannot catch him. There are four principles that you must know to apply kung-fu effectively. They are:

一、以靜待動 夫動則氣浮，靜則神定。以靜待動，彼則竭而我盈，所謂先發制人，未有不反為人所制也。

1. Using passive inaction to wait and counter the opponent's action (attack).

When the opponent moves hastily, his chi will rise. If you are passive, then you will be alert and attentive. Use inactive passiveness to wait for the opponent to act first. Then the opponent will be open to a counter while you are fully covered (protected). This is what the saying, "those who attack first will only be defeated," means.

二、以柔濟剛 災炎者滅，燒匕者缺。齒以剛折，舌以柔存。彼身可合圍，力能扛鼎，而我一挑半剗已挫折有余矣。

2. Use gentleness to conquer hardness.

The razing fire is quickly destroyed. The tooth is easily broken because it is hard. It is hard to destroy the tongue because it is soft. The opponent may be robust and have the strength to lift a tripod. But with a flick and slash technique, you can easily defeat him.

三、以速御遲　秦中逐鹿，捷足先得，況兩雄相角，勝負轉瞬間乎。惟電閃風行，靜如處女，出如脫兔，是非笨伯所能當也。

3. Use speed to control the slower opponent.

The speedy runner arrives first. When two strong fighters engage in combat, victory is determined within a fraction of a second, like the speed of lightning and the blowing rage of the wind. Be passive like a lady. But if you move, be as agile as a rabbit. This is beyond the skill of a clumsy person.

四、以虛擊實　將欲取之，必姑與之。欲將與之，必姑棄之。出不急以攻無備，此柔術不二法門也。虛與委蛇，俾應接不暇，而吾技進矣。夫柔術錯綜變化，自非筆墨所能形容，而能動中機宜，箭無虛發吾知其必有合也。

4. Feint before you strike. Be deceptive.

If you plan to get in, pretend that you are not interested. If your intention is to get out, pretend that you want to get in. Don't show your intention to attack so that you can catch him off guard. Pretend to be relaxed so when you suddenly approach him, this is the proper time to attack. There are so many possibilities and changes when using this gentle art that the pen cannot fully describe them all. Act when a favorable opportunity arises. Don't move aimlessly. Then you can manipulate the situation to your liking.

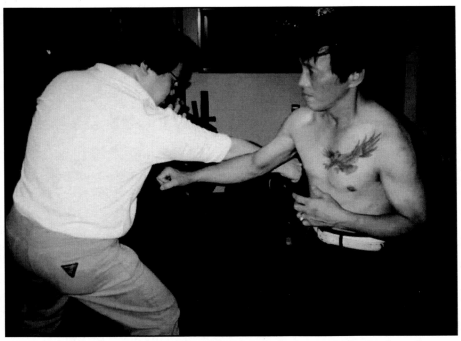

Ang Hua Kun striking Alexamder Co's ribs from outside bridge (1994).

3 GENTLE ART POSTURES
柔術之姿勢

柔術首重姿勢，無姿勢則如傀儡之登場。雖亦布亦趨，旅進旅退，索然無復生氣矣。是故

Proper posture is the first requirement of this gentle art. Without proper posture, you will be like a puppet pulled by a string. Even though you can move around and back and forth, still you will resemble a dummy. You will lack any trace of life and gracefulness. Such that:

百會提則頭挺，牙關起而項強
When you perform, you should hold your head erect.
Pull your mouth down, to strengthen your neck.

耳聽八方，眼光四射
The ears should be attentive, in order to sense the eight directions.
The eyes should be sharp, in order to cover the four ways.

兩肩墜而心胸守，十趾翹則足力生
Both shoulders should sink down, to protect the chest.
The toes should curl up, to give power to the legs.

步武注重後枝，運功先提五肚
In moving your stances, emphasis is put on the back leg.
Before you emit power, you should first inhale and lift your five organs.

卸大椎以通中氣，兜前足以故膀胱
Keep your spine straight and curl in at the coccyx, so that the chi can flow smoothly.
Invert your front leg, to cover the groin.

小腹須防，尾閭務夾
Tighten the lower stomach. Tuck the coccyx.

此則全身之姿勢，習柔術者不可不知也。至若舉重若輕，膽前在後，安如磐石，矯若游龍，出沒無端，隨機應變。

This is the proper posture that practitioners of this art should know. Thus, when you are faced with any undertaking, big or small, you will have full confidence. This will enable you to be as solid as a rock and as agile as a dragon. There will be no mistakes in your techniques and you will be able to counter any attack.

孫思邈曰：膽欲大而心欲小，智欲圓而行欲方，神而明知存乎其人矣。

"Only courage is necessary, even if your heart is small. Wisdom will help you conquer your enemies, for when you have self-control and wisdom you can know your enemies."—*Sun Simiao*

GENTLE ART OPENING METHOD
柔術開始法

請拳姿勢
SALUTATION POSTURES

立正姿勢。如體操法
Stand Erect - Stand at attention as in physical exercise.

雙曲手從立正夾拳手曲之，而掌心對肩。
Double Bending Arm (*sang ow chiu*) – From the Stand Erect, bend both arms with the palms facing toward the shoulders. Close the fists and pull them up.

雙壓手從曲手，退右足平馬，同時壓下。
Double Pressing Hand (*sang an chiu*) – From Double Bending Arm, step with the right leg into a level horse stance and press down.

雙擒手從壓下之勢，而轉雙擒至眉上，即美女梳妝。
Double Grabbing Hand (*sang kim chiu*) – From the Double Pressing Hand posture, swing both hands into a double grab at eyebrow level. This is also called, "Beauty Fixing Her Makeup" (*be li suey tzun*).

抱印手從雙擒扭右側，即關平抱印。
Holding the Seal (*po in chiu*) – From the Double Grabbing Hand, pull the right fist in toward your right side. Cover it with the left palm. This is also called, "Guan Ping Holding the Seal" (*guan ping po in*).

請拳手從抱印請至中，即將軍抱印。
Salutation Fist (*chia kun*) – From Holding the Seal posture, extend both hands to the middle. This is also called, "General Holding the Seal" (*jong gun po en*).

坐節手從請拳，坐節於側下，即頓手。
Sinking the Wrist (*che chat*) – From the Salutation Fist, open the hands and sink the wrists to the sides. Keep arms extended to the front. This is also called, "Trembling Hand" (*tun chu*).

雙吞手從坐節吞至兩肩外，掌心向後方，即白鶴展翅。
Double Swallowing Hand (*sang chun chiu*) – From the Sinking Wrist, bring your hands back to the sides of your shoulders, palms facing backward. This is the *swallowing* movement. This is also called, "White Crane Spreads Its Wings" (*pe ho tian sit*).

雙駿手從吞手吐至兩側下，即迫肶駿肶
Double Vibrating Hand (*sang tun chiu*) – From the Swallowing Hand posture, *spit* the hands out to the front. Keep both hands separate. This is also called, "Press Stomach" (*piak to*) and "Vibrate Stomach" (*chun to*).

即請拳一定之開始法
STANDARD SALUTE FOR THE OPENING METHOD

Editor's Note: The salutation, formally known as the "qi kun" or "commencement fist," is the starting method of Ngo Cho Kun. It is the opening salutation set that begins every empty-hand form and partner training set within the system. More than just a bow, it is a structure-tested series of movements that has within it the four main concepts of the art: pu (float), tim (sink), tun (swallow), and toh (spit out). For some reason, Yu Chiok Sam gave it two entries in this book. For continuity, we have combined the smaller entries into this combined single section.

立正
Stand Erect

雙手曲
Bend Both Hands

退平馬同時兩手壓下
Step with the right leg into level horse stance, press down with both hands

雙擒至眉
Execute double grab (*kim*) with both hands to eyebrow level

扭右側抱印
Twist to the right side, with "holding the seal" posture (see detail)

請拳
The Salutation

坐節
Bend and sink the wrist joints (*che chat*)

吞手過肩外
Swallow hands (*tun chiu*)

駿手兩下
Vibrate the hands (*chun chiu*) down from both sides

5	**GENTLE ART CLOSING METHOD**
	柔術完全法

Editor's Note: *As with the Opening Method, Yu Chiok Sam also presented the Closing Method in two different sections of the book. For continuity, we have combined these sections into one, more comprehensive presentation.*

收拳姿勢 - CLOSING FIST POSTURES

"Enticing Hand" Closing Posture - *Chiao Yong Chiu*

如尾技手轉破者，直退寄右足收招陽手。招陽手從轉破之勢，直退寄右足。收兩手坐節於右側，即雙掛手，並釵手、手抱牌立正。

If the last of the techniques is the ***rotating chop*** (*tsuan puah*), step directly back and close with the ***enticing hand*** (*chiao yong chiu*). From the rotating chop posture, step straight back, hanging the right foot. Retract both hands while sinking the wrists at your right side. This is also called the ***double hanging hand*** (*sang kwa chiu*). Extend both hands forward into the ***enticing hand*** posture.

Ending in Rotating Chop (*tsuan puah*)   Angle Perspective

Enticing Hand (*chao yong chiu*) Closing Posture   Angle Perspective

"Holding the Tablet" Closing Posture - *Po Pai*

其拳手，釵手收抱牌手。立正曲手，並垂下。

If the last of the techniques is a **punch** (*kun chiu*) or a **side thrust** (*tueh chiu*), close with **holding the tablet** (*po pai*). Stand erect, bend both hands, and drop them down.

Ending in Punch

Ending in Side Thrust

Holding the Tablet (*po pai*) Closing Posture

雙舉手從立正舉之，而收曲肩，並十字擋，雙垂下。十字擋從雙曲手。擋出左右平伸。即收拳之運動法。

Double Lifting Hands (*sang gi chiu*) – From the **standing erect** posture, lift the hands and bend them near the shoulder. Deliver a cross thrust, then drop both arms.

Cross Pattern Thrust (*sip li t'ng*) - From the **double lifting hands**, thrust out both left and right downward, stretching out equally. This is the closing movement of the exercise method.

Double Lifting Hands

Cross (Elbow) Thrust

Lower Hands

6 HAND AND STEP COORDINATION METHOD
柔術順步法

Editor's Note: *It is very easy in martial arts to get distracted by memorizing sequences within the forms. Practitioners forget there is more to a punch than just the punch itself. In Ngo Cho Kun the important pieces of techniques come in the form of maxims, or phrases that give direction and meaning to movements and technqiues. In this section, Yu Chiok Sam set out the maxims for coordinating the hand and foot movements.*

如左腳跨出左手隨之，右腳跨出右手隨之，

If you step out with your left leg, the left hand should follow. If you step out with your right leg, the right hand should follow.

無論左右之動作，總以到足亦到，

When you move either right or left, the hands and feet should act as one unit,

五枝齊動，從後腳發力，

using the "five parts power" *(ngo ki lat)*, where power starts from the heel of the back leg.

如弓箭步丁八馬，

For example, take the bow-and-arrow character T stance *(king tzi bo ting pat be)*. (***Editor's note:*** *this stance is commonly known as chien be ("battle horse")* 戰馬).

未發力者，寄步丁字馬，

Before you emit power, stand in the hanging leg character T stance *(kia ka ting li be)*.

跨步前足四分馬，後腳六分力，

When you step forward keep 40-percent of your body weight on the front leg and 60-percent on the rear leg.

手勢擊出七分力，扭入三同時發

When your hands strike out, use 70-percent of your power to strike out and pull in your other hand with the remaining 30-percent.

足部大約相距二尺為步。

Stances are approximately two feet apart. The stances are:

Character	Hokkien	English Description
直馬	Tit Be	Straight Horse Stance
弓箭步	Kieng Tzi Po	Bow and Arrow Stance
丁八步	Ting Pat Po	"丁" and "八" - shaped Stance
角馬	Kak Be	Angle Horse Stance
寄足馬	Kia Ka Be	Hanging Foot Stance
丁字馬	Ting Li Be	"丁" - shaped Stance
平馬	Pi Be	Level Horse Stance
八字步	Pat Li Po	"八" - shaped Stance
橫塌馬	Hui Tap Be	Horizontal Overlapping Step
反弓馬	Wan Kieng Be	Reverse Bow Stance

者隨技手之變通焉。

Coordinate the stances with the hand techniques.

位置之大小，如人行步前足兜，是為直馬、丁八馬。

The length of the stance is similar to the length of a stride as you walk. The front leg is turned inward. This is the ***straight horse*** *(tit be),* 丁 ***and*** 八 ***character stance*** *(ting pat be),* halfway between the Chinese character for 8 and the Roman letter T, and is like a triangle in shape. (***Editor's Note:*** *Going forward, we will refer to this stance as chian be* 戰馬).

再退一足位為角馬、丁字步。　又退平是為八字馬或橫馬。

Retreat one leg and face the corner. This is the **Angle Stance** (*kak be*). Retreat one more to a level position into a character **"8"- Shaped Stance** (*ba tzi be*) or a **Horizontal Stance** (*hui be*).

直進步提前足跨一步，同時後足進立如弓箭步。前足力四分，後足力六分。

Straight Forward Step (*tit chin po*) – Lift the front leg and take one step forward. The rear leg also steps forward and stands in the ***bow and arrow stance*** (*king tzi po*). The front leg bears 40% and the rear leg 60% of the weight.

直退步提後足退一步，同時前足退立如寄足馬。前足力三分，後足力七分。

Straight Backward Step (*tit teh po*) – Lift the rear leg and step backward. The front leg follows and stands in the ***hanging leg*** (*kia ka be*) stance. The front leg bears 30% and the rear leg 70% of the weight.

踏足步提後足跨前一步，同時兩足兜轉丁八馬，如弓箭步。

Stepping On (*ta ka po*) – Step forward with the rear leg and simultaneously tuck in both legs in a **Battle Stance** (*chien be, ting pat be*) or **Bow and Arrow Stance** (*king tzi po*).

退足步提前足退後一步，同時兩足如前法。

Stepping Back (*teh ka po*) – Step back with the front leg and simultaneously tuck in both legs as in the previous method.

平馬步提前足退平，向左向右隨技手之變法。

Level Step (*ping be po*) – Step back with the front leg into a parallel position. Then turn to either right or left according to the hand technique.

換馬步提前足收平如立正，同時後足跨出如寄足步。

Changing Step (*hua-be po*) – Lift the front leg and retreat into a parallel position as if standing with feet together. The rear leg then slides forward into a hanging leg.

翻轉步如右足在前，移位於左角一步，同時左轉翻後。左足在前移位於右角一步，同時右轉翻前，右足在前閃角向左畔，踏角翻右畔，再閃角向前，收左足立正。

Turning Pivot Step (*huan tuan po*) – Drill: If the right leg is forward, shift it to your left corner and pivot toward your left as you turn to face the rear. Now the left leg is forward; shift it to your right corner and simultaneously pivot toward your right as you turn to face the front. Then, with the right leg forward, shift toward the left corner and face toward your left side. Then, again shift to the corner as you turn to face the rear. Retract your left leg. Stand at attention.

寄足步丁字馬。前足力三分，後足力七分。兩股吞平前足寄。

Hanging Foot Step, T-Shaped Stance (*kia ka po, ding li be*) – The front leg bears 30% and the rear leg bears 70% of the weight. Both thighs face to the front and are positioned parallel to the front leg as it hangs in the stance.

弓箭步八字馬。前足力四分，後足力六分。兩股吞平前足兜。如反弓馬者，前後之力對反而。

Bow and Arrow Step, "8"-Shaped Stance (*king tzi po, pat li be*) – The front leg bears 40% and the rear leg bears 60% of the weight. Both thighs are positioned parallel to the front tucked-in leg and face front. If in a reversed bow stance, the weight distribution is reversed.

Front   *Reverse*

踏轉步如右足在前，踏左足一步，同時右轉翻後。

Advancing Pivot Step (*ta tzuan po*) – If the right leg is forward, step forward with the left leg and turn toward your right to face the rear.

榻轉步如右足在前，盤踏向後，跨左足動作。在盤踏左足向前，夸右足動作，即榻馬步。

Overlapping Step and Turn (*tap tzuan po*) – If the right leg is forward, cross it over your left leg while stepping to the rear and step forward with the left leg. Then cross your left leg over your right toward your front and simultaneously step forward with the right leg. This is the ***overlapping step*** (*tap be po*).

疊進步如右足在前，跨左足一步，同時跨右足動作，即雙進。

Continuous Forward Step (*tiap chin po*) - If the right leg is forward, step forward with the left leg and follow with a right step forward. The right leg should be forward. This is also called the **double step forward** (*sang chin*).

疊退步如右足在前，退後一步，同時退右足動作，即雙退。

Continuous Backward Step (*tiap teh po*) – If the right leg is forward, step back one step. The left leg follows with a step backward. This is also called the ***double step backward*** (*sang teh*).

走馬步跨左角一步，同時跨右角，向右動作。

Walking Step (*cho be po*) – Step diagonally into the left corner and, at the same time, step into the right corner as you move. One leg should always be ahead of the other. This is also known as ***diagonal stepping***.

鈎角法：提右足鈎人前足，直退鈎之令仆。如敵人先鈎於我者，同時跨後足一步擋之。

Hooking Method (*gao ka wat*) – Lift your right leg and hook your opponent's front leg from the inside. Step back as you hook in order to make him stumble. If the opponent hooks you first, take one step back to counter with a ***palm strike*** (*t'ng chiu*).

榻腳法：提右足榻人右足後，並擋以倒之。

Overlapping Leg Method (*tap ka wat*) – Lift the right leg and overlap it over the back of the opponent's right leg. Pull back your right leg and thrust simultaneously with your ***palm*** (*t'ng chiu*) in order to topple him.

掃腿法：提右足掃人前足，使猝不及防。

Sweeping Leg Method (*sao ka wat*) – Lift your right leg and sweep your opponent's front leg in order to catch him unawares.

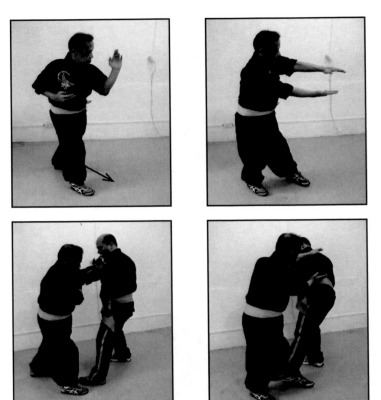

拔腳法即截腳，提左足拔人右足後，並雙批之

Pulling Leg Method (*pueh ka wat*) or **Intercepting Leg** (*jeet ka*) – Lift your left leg and pull or hook the back of your opponent's right leg. Execute a **double slap hand** (*sang pueh*).

跶腳法：全身坐力在後足，提前足吊至膀胱下，跶出與臍平。

(Front) Kicking Technique (*tat ka wat*) – Put your entire weight on your rear leg and lift the front leg so it hangs near your crotch. Kick out to navel height.

駿腳法：提前足，駿跶敵人之膝蓋或足後。

(Side) Vibrating Kick (*chun ka wat*) – Lift your front leg and kick your opponent's kneecap or the back of his leg.

閃身屈觀來勢正銳，閃左右以避其鋒。

Evading Body Kneeling (*siam sin kut*) – Upon observing that the opponent is charging in fiercely, evade to either side to avoid his attack.

力士擋用右手栓人足膝，左手並擋之。

Strong Man Thrust (*lek si t'ng*) – Use your right hand to catch your opponent's knee and thrust with your left palm.

屈馬擋即落地折筍，進屈右足擋人膝蓋，
左手掀之。

Kneeling Stance Thrust (*kut be t'ng*) – also called
kneeling down to bend the bamboo shoots (*lo the at tiak soon*). Step into a kneeling stance so your right palm thrusts into your opponent's kneecap while your left hand grabs it.

☒攦屈向左屈之，左手擒人之右手，同時右手鈎人
足後。

Double Split Kneeling Hand (*sang li chiu*) – As you kneel to the left, grab the opponent's right hand with your left hand, and at the same time use your right hand to hook the back of his leg.

開弓屈退左右足屈之，以避敵人飛趌也。

Pulling Bow Kneeling (*kwi kieng kut*) – Step back with either leg to kneel down in order to avoid your opponent's kick.

坐蓮屈退左足榻坐後，呈轉雙扭趌，即坐禪步。

Sitting Lotus Kneeling (*che lien kut*) – Step back with your left leg inserted behind your right leg as you squat down. As you rise up, double grab and kick. It is also called **sitting zen step**.

穿腳法即海底穿針，提左足穿人股下，並盤左轉向後，裟鞭。

Piercing Feet Method (*chuan ka wat*) – also called **Sea Bottom Piercing Needle** (*hai tue chun cham*). Lift your left leg and insert it beneath your opponent's thigh and twist toward your left as you turn back to **grasp and backfist** (*sha pien*).

倒剪法提左足趺人股下並倒左側盤剪，反剪鈎趺。

Falling Scissor Method (*to chian wat*) – Lift your left leg to kick your opponent's lower thigh, then slide down to your left side as you scissor him. Then reverse scissor and hook and kick.

屈馬即向天獅，進右足屈之而駿敵人右擊手。屈馬擒者，進右足左手擒上，右手扭人之膝令仆。

Kneeling Stance Grab (*kut be so*) / **Facing the Sky Lion** (*hiong tien tsai*) – Step forward with the right leg. Kneel down and grab your opponent's attacking hand. Kneeling grab. Step forward with right foot. The left hand grabs upward and the right hand pulls or grabs the opponent's knee to topple him.

指地屈，如敵人用足穿我股下，同時壓之，即蟾蜍翁

Point at the Ground Kneeling (*tzi teh kut*) – If the opponent uses his leg to insert between your thighs, press down with your knee. This is also known as **the spider**.

鞭 - Pian
Whip/Backfist

踏右足右手從肩上。笑手鞭人面部。

With the right foot forward, back-fist downward from the shoulder into your opponent's face.

貢手 - Kong Chiu
Hammer Hand

踏右足右手豎拳貢中。
即 打手。

With the right foot forward, use a vertical fist. Hammer strike toward the center. This is also called the **shocking hand** (*pa chiu*).

沉手 - Tim Chiu
Sinking Hand

踏右足覆手拳打下。即 鐵槌。

With the right foot forward, use an inverted fist and punch downward. This is also called the **heavy hammer sinking** (*ti tue tim*).

打節 - **Pa Chat**
Elbow Strike

踏右足右手擊人胸部。
左手夾之。

With the right foot forward, use the elbow to strike the opponent's chest. Clip your left hand to the elbow.

刈節 - **Kua Chat**
Reaping Elbow

踏右足右手刈人。
左手折斷。

With the right foot forward, the right elbow smashes into the opponent's left hand in order to break it.

擒手 - **Kim Chiu - Grabbing Hand**

踏右足從左側下擒上。如五爪之勢。

With the right foot forward, the right hand comes up from the left side and swings up to grab in a five finger claw formation.

盤手 - Pua Chiu - Entangling Hand

踏左足左手擒。右手並挑之。而雙掛入。

With the left foot forward, the left hand **grabs** (*kim*) and the right hand **flick blocks** (*tioh*). Then strike out with a **double palm thrust** (*sang kwa lip*).

啄手- Tok Chiu
Poking Hand

如踏右足。
右手從左側下啄人胸部。

With the right foot forward, the right hand comes up from the left side and pokes into the oponent's chest.

盖手 - Kay Chiu
Scooping Hand

如踏右足。
右手從左肩上盖下。

With the right foot forward, the right hand scoops downward from the left shoulder.

挑手 - **Tioh Chiu**
Flicking Hand

如踏右足。
右手從左側下挑上。

With the right foot forward, flick
or swing the right hand upward
from the left side.

掀手 - **Hian Chiu**
Turning Hand

如踏右足。
右手掀敵人上擊手。

With the right foot forward, turn
to block the opponent's upper gate
attack.

鈎搖 - **Kao Yao**
Hook and Shake

如踏左足。
左手鈎下　右手搖上。

With the left foot forward, hook
downward with the left hand and
swing upward with the right hand
to strike.

撟手- Kiao Chiu
Uppercut

如踏右足。右手垂後。夾豎
拳。撟人股下。

With right foot forward, swing
the right hand upward in a vertical
fist position. The hand comes up
from the rear. Uppercut is aimed
between your opponent's thighs.

Front Uppercut　　　　*Side Uppercut*

窕肩 - Tiao Kian
Side Shoulder

平馬向左畔。右手如擒勢插
前。閃人擊手。

Assume a bow-and-arrow stance
facing left. The right hand **grabs**
(*kim*) then thrusts forward, ending
as an upper strike.

按手 - An Chiu
Pressing Hand

與人掀手不動者。前手串上而
坐節。並梱之。

If unable to **turn** (*hian*) an opponent's hand, the right hand should
pierce upward. **Sink the wrist** (*che
chiat*) and then do an **entwining**
(*tin*) maneuver.

貫中 - Kwan Tiong
Center Thrust

踏右足。兩手從左側下。
夾笑手拳。擊人胸部。

With the right foot forward, both hands uppercut forward from the left side into the opponent's chest.

托手 - Tuh Chiu
Lifting Hand

者托人牙關。

The lifting hand is used to strike upward at the opponent's jaw.

Lifting Hand - Punch   *Lifting Hand - Palm*

接手 - Chiap Chiu - Connecting Hand

兩人踏右足角馬。右手貫中以鼻爲子午。

Both feet step forward with the right leg forward. The right fist thrusts up to the nose in an outer guard position.

單手插 - Tan Chiu Cha
Single Thrust

如踏右足。右手插人胸部。

If the right leg is forward, the right hand thrusts to the opponent's chest.

反馬插 - Wan Be Cha
Reverse Thrust

如踏左足。右手插下。
掌心向外。

If the left leg is forward, the right hand thrusts down, palm facing outside.

標插 - Pio Cha
Throwing Thrust

如踏左足。右手插下。　標插向內。

If the left leg is forward, the right hand thrusts down, palm facing inward.

Editor's Note: *Photos match technique names, but not descriptions, perhaps due to typsetting error in original.*

單手拳 - Tan Chiu Kun
Single Punch

如踏右足。右手擊人胸部。拇指夾食指中節。

If the right leg is forward, use the right fist to punch the opponent's chest. The thumb is clenched in at the forefinger.

反馬拳 - Wan Be Kun
Reverse Punch

如踏左足。右手擊人丹田。掌心向外。即 虎馬拳。

If the left leg is forward, the right fist punches at the opponent's *dantien*. The palm should face outward. This is also called the **tiger stance fist** (*ho be kun*) 虎馬拳.

擋手 - T'ng Chiu
Palm Thrust

即雙印掌。如踏右足。右手擊人胸部。

Also called **pressing palm**, if the right leg is forward, strike the opponent's chest with right palm.

切手 - Chiat Chiu
Slice Chop

即切人肩上截手。

This is used to slice/chop the opponent's shoulder.

截 - Chà
Intercept Chop

即截人肕邊。

The intercept chop is used to chop the side of the opponent's stomach.

釵手 - Tueh Chiu
Side Thrust

如衝拳勢。
用右手釵人胸部。

Thrust the right palm into the opponent's chest, as in a punch.

開手 - Kai Chiu
Downward Block

如踏右足。右手從左肩上開
下。

If the right hand is forward, block
down from the left shoulder.

反馬搖 - Wan Be Yao
Reverse Shaking Hand

反馬搖者掌心向出。

In the reverse shaking hand, the
palm faces outward.

反弓手 - Wan Kieng Chiu
Reverse Bow Hand

如前手開下。後手扭入。
即 白馬射。

Also called *white horse shooting
arrow*, this is similar to the *downward block* (kai), but the other
hand pulls in.

破手 - Puah Chiu
Downward Chop

即 斬手。右手從肩上破下。

Also called the ***cutting hand*** (斬手 *cham chiu*). The right hand chops down from the shoulder.

轉破 - Tsuan Puah - Rotating Chop

右手從左肩破中。並收招揚手。

The right hand chops down from the left shoulder. Then execute the ***enticing hand*** (*chiao yong chiu*) to close.

抄鞭手- Sha Pian Chiu
Grasp and Whip

踏左足。左手如擒勢拖人。
同時右手鞭出。

Step forward with the left leg. The left hand ***grabs*** (*kim*), and pulls inward, while the right hand strikes out in a ***backfist*** (*pian*).

鈎打手 - Kon Ta Chiu
Hooking Strike Hand

如踏左角。左手鈎下。
同時右手打上。

If you are standing in a left angle/corner stance, the left hand **hooks down** (*kao*), and the right palm simultaneously strikes in an **upward chop** (*ta*).

鳳眼手 - Hong Gan Chiu
Phoenix Eye Fist

如班指勢。打人太陽穴。

Extend out the forefinger (knuckle) and use it to strike the opponent's temple cavity.

牛角兜 - Gu Kak Tao
Cow Horn

牛角兜用豎拳。

The cow horn uses a vertical fist.

雙挑手 - Sang Tioh Chiu
Double Flicking Hand

從下挑上。並坐節。

From below, flick both hands upward. Then sink the wrists.

雙鈎手 - Sang Kao Chiu
Double Hooking Hand

從上鈎下。並按手。

From above, hook down. Then do a **press hand** (*an chiu*).

雙搖手 - Sang Yao Chiu
Double Shaking Hand

從後而 搖前。並雙鈎。

From the back, swing the hands toward the front and then go into a **double hook** (*sang kao*).

雙撟手 - Sang Kiao Chiu
Double Uppercut

用拳手。撟人丹田。

Using both fists, uppercut into your opponent's *dantien*.

雙盖手 - Sang Kay Chiu
Double Scooping Hand

從上盖至兩側下。

Scoop the hands toward the sides of the body.

雙掇節 - Sang Kwa Chat
Double Plucking Elbow

從雙撟掇兩肩外。

From the double uppercut, pluck the elbows outward from the shoulder.

葫蘆手 - O-Lo Chiu
Urn Hand / Gourd Hand

葫蘆手用平拳。

The urn hand uses a flat fist to strike at the opponent's waist.

雙破手 - Sang Puah Chiu
Double Chopping Hand

從肩上破下。

From the shoulder, chop down. This is also called the **cutting hand** (*cham chiu* 斬手).

雙貢手 - Sang Kong Chiu
Double Hammerstrike

用豎拳打中。

Using the vertical fist position, strike down toward the center. This is also called the **double striking hand** (*sang ta chiu* 雙打手).

雙扯剪 - Sang Chi Chian
Double Scissors

踏右足。右手從肩上。
左手垂下。同時剪之。

If the right leg is forward, the right hand should come from the shoulder and the left hand should come from your side. Bring them to the center, execute the scissors.

雙關剪 - Sang Kwi Chian
Double Closing Scissors

踏右足。兩手夾敵人之手折
斷。

With the right foot forward, both hands clip to scissors position and break your opponent's hand.

雙摛手 - Sang Li Chiu
Double Split

向左向右。前手如擒後手鈎
下。

Split toward the left and the right. The front hand assumes the *grab* (kim), while the rear hand assumes the **hook** (kao).

雙梭手 - Sang So Chiu - Double Grabbing Hand

即 虎頭揢 踏右足右手如擒勢。左手如之。而扭躂。

Also called the ***tiger head hold*** (*ho tao so* 虎頭揢). Step forward with the right foot. The right hand **grabs** (*kim*), with the left hand assisting. Then ***wrench*** (*liu*) and kick (*ta*).

抱盤揢 - Po Pua So
Holding the Tray Grab

如退右足右手拖人右手。左手
並扭之。以使其仆

If retreating with the right foot, the hand pulls your opponent's right hand, with the left hand ***wrenching*** (*liu*) or twisting. This is also for throwing the opponent.

雙扭手 - San Liu Chiu - Double Twisting / Wrenching Hand

從雙批之。並扭躂。

From the ***double slapping hand*** (*sang pueh chiu*), ***wrench*** (*liu*) then ***kick*** (*ta*).

**雙捲手 - Sang K'n Chiu
Double Coiling Hand**

即 茵藤籐。並雙彈。

Also called ***entwining hand*** (*in tin chiu* 茵籐手). Immediately ***double spring chop*** (*sang tua*).

抱牌手 - Po Pai Chiu
Holding the Tablet Hand

如踏右足右手盖下。左手擋人胸部。

Step forward with the right foot. The right hand **scoops down** (*kay*), and the left hand strikes out at the opponent's chest.

和手擒 - Ho Chiu Kim
Assisted Grab

踏右足右手如擒。左手隨之。即 鳳尾彩。又名雙押。

With the right foot forward, the right hand **grabs** (*kim*) and the left hand assists. This is also called the **elegant phoenix tail** (*hong be tsai*) and **double cap** (*sang tao*).

和手挑 - Ho Chiu Tioh
Assisted Flicking Hand

踏右足 兩手從左側下挑至右肩上

With the right foot forward, both flick upward from the left toward your shoulder.

和手掀 - Ho Chiu Hian
Assisted Turning Hand

和手從左側下　用拳手掀上

Both hands execute **turning hand** (*hian*) from the left side using the fists.

和手鈎 - Ho Chiu Kao
Assisted Hook

踏右足　兩手從上而鈎下

With the right foot forward, both hands hook downward from above.

反墜手 - Wan Twi Chiu - Reverse Falling Hand

從打節　反右手鞭人面部

From the **elbow strike** (*pa chat*), **backfist** (*wan twi chiu*) toward the opponent's face.

DOUBLE LONG-HAND TECHNIQUES
雙手長機

雙掛手 - Sang Kwa Chiu
Double Hanging Thrust

同時出者。即雙掛手。

If both hands attack simultaneously, it is called a **double hanging thrust** (*sang kwa chiu*).

雙豎插 - Sang Kia Cha
Double Vertical Thrust

兩手從胸前。插與平肩。
拇指夾掌心。四指垂下。

From the chest, thrust both arms toward the front at shoulder level. Clip the thumbs into the center of the palms. The four fingers should point down.

雙陰插 - Sang Yim Cha
Double Yin Thrust

兩手扭胸側。插與平肩。
掌心向下。即 雙平插。

Also called the **double flat thrust**, twist both arms beside your chest. Thrust out at shoulder level, palms facing down.

雙擋手 - Sang T'ng Chiu
Double Palm Thrust

即雙印掌。從兩側擋與平肩。
並扭之。

Also called **pressing palm**, from both sides, thrust out at shoulder level then slowly close your grip in a **wrenching** maneuver (*liu*).

雙拳手 - Sang Kun Chiu
Double Punch

從兩側。擊人胸部。
拇指夾食指中。

From both sides, strike out toward your opponent's chest. Clench the thumb at the forefinger.

雙豎拳 - Sang Kia Kun
Double Vertical Fist

如踏右足。右手上拳。
左手下拳。

If the right leg is forward, the right fist punches upward and the left fist punches down.

雙彈手 - Sang Tua Chiu
Double Spring Hand

從左肩上。彈人胸部。
右上左下。

From the left shoulder, spring out, hitting your opponent's chest. The right hand goes over the left.

雙批拳 - Sang Pueh Chiu
Double Slap Hand

如踏右足。
兩手從左肩上。
批對肩平。

If the right leg is forward, slap both hands down to shoulder level, starting from the left shoulder.

雙開搖 - Sang Kai Yao
Double Block and Shake

如踏右足。右手開下。
同時左手搖上。

If the right leg is forward, the right hand **blocks downward** (*kai*) and the left hand simultaneously **swings upward** (*yao*).

雙墜拳 - Sang Tui Kun
Double Falling Punch

兩手擊人丹田下。拳背相向。

Use both hands to strike at your opponent's *dantien*. The back of the fists should face in the same direction.

雙串拳 - Sang Ch'ng Kun
Double Piercing Fist

從雙墜串上。解敵人束腰法。

From the double downward fist posture (*sang tui kun*), pierce upwards. This is used for breaking loose when someone grabs your waist.

Editor's Note: *While we don't know for certain who developed the Kao Tuan Kim Wat, it is assumed that since Ngo Cho Kun's founder, Chua Giok Beng, oversaw the writing of this book by Yu Chiok Sam, that it is from Chua himself. Please note, that this Nine Section Brocade Method is not related to the popular Eight Section Brocade Qigong set known as Ba Duan Jin. These are a series of short fighting sets that place little direct emphasis on chi development.*

A brocade is a richly decorative class of interwoven and embroidered colorful silken fabrics. In this spirit, the Nine Section Brocade Method is actually made up of a collection of Ngo Cho Kun special techniques, connected or woven together to make up short training drills. Most of these methods are just extractions from sequences found within the 38 forms (roads) described later in this book. These short combination sets are devices that enable students to advance their skills without having first to learn all 38 forms, making the Nine Section Brocade a sort of short cut drill.

In Chinese numerology, the number nine represents tonification, infinity. This is how the Nine Section Brocade should be practiced: as an endless combination of offensive and defensive techniques, intricately interwoven and connected. The reader will notice that actually there are 10 sections in total, though still being referred to as "nine sections." This is because the number 10 in Chinese has an antonym that sounds like death. So nine is used in the title of the drilling method, while there are actually 10 sections in total.

Pictorial Overview of the Kau Tuan Kim Wat

寄左足，左手夾右側上，右手起吊於額頂五寸，兩掌心向外。

Left Hanging Leg. The left hand is tucked near your right side. The right hand lifts up, five inches above your forehead. Both hands face palm outward.

練習法 - Training Method:

立正。請。坐節。退右足屈左手開。呈身擒。踏右足右手撟。退右足羅漢手。並左手挑。換右足挑。並屈手開弓。呈身右手擒。直進翻後屈左手開。如前法。翻前至右手擒。收立正曲手並垂下。

Stand in attention stance. Salutation bow, *che chat*. Step back with right leg into *kut be*. Left hand *kai*. Rise up and left hand *kim*. Step forward with the right leg and execute a right *kiao*. Step back with the right leg into the *lohan chiu*, then execute a left *tioh*. *Hua be* into right lead and execute a right *tioh*. Then left *kut be* and *kwe kieng*. Rise up while executing a right hand *kim*. Step straight forward and turn to face the rear. Drop into a left *kut be* and left hand *kai*. Repeat the sequence until you turn to face the front. Continue up to the right hand *kim*. Close. As you stand in attention, pull both arms to the side as you drop them.

魁星手法 - Kwi Seng Chiu Wat
GOD OF LITERATURE HAND METHOD

退左足榻後，左手夾右側下，右手串上，掌心向內。

Step back with left leg leg crossing behind right, left hand tucks under and across the right side of the chest. The right hand pushes upward, elbow bent, in the form of phoenix eye fist (*hong ngan chiu*). Both palms face inward.

練習法 - Training Method:

退榻左足。魁星手。進左手挑。並開。踏右足屈右手擋。呈身擒。退右足左手擒。踏右足雙掛入。直進榻向後魁星手。進左手挑。並開。直右足屈右手擋。呈身擒。退右足左手擒。踏右足雙掛入。直進榻向前魁星手。進左手挑。換右足右手轉破。收立正。

Step back with left leg into *tap be po* and execute the *Kwi Seng chiu*. Step forward with the left leg and execute a left *tioh* then do a *kai*. Step foreward with right leg into *kut be* and execute right *t'ng*. Rise up and do a right *kim*. Step back with the right leg, left hand *kim*. Step forward with the right leg and do a *sang kwi lip*. Step straight forward crossing the left under the right so you turn to face the rear. The right leg overlaps the left. Execute *Kwi Seng chiu*. Step forward as left hand executes a *tioh* and *kai*. Step forward with the right leg and do a right *t'ng*. Rise up and do a right *kim*. Step back with the right leg and do a left *kim*. Step forward with right leg and do a *sang kwa lip*. Step straight forward while doing a *tap be po* so you turn facing toward the front. Execute *Kwi Seng chiu*. Step forward with the left leg and do a left hand *tioh*. Shift to the right leg and do a right *puah*. Close. Stand in attention stance.

猴挑水法 - Gao Tioh Sui Wat
MONKEY FLICKING WATER METHOD

即側插，從吞手插出左右平伸。

This is also called **side thrust** (*chia cha*). From the swallowing hand, thrust out toward right and left sides.

練習法 - Training Method:

平馬雙墜。吞手。側插。坐節。再吞手。側插。坐節。踏右足雙撟。雙盖。鳳眼手。平馬左手盖。右手刈。右手盖。左手刈。跳進左足指地。閃右手挑。左手挑。呈身右手切。並屈開弓。呈身左手擒。換右手破。收立正。

Step forward with left leg into a *pi be* stance. Thrust both hands downward. Execute a *tun chiu*, a *chia chat*, and then *che chiat*. Repeat the *tun chiu*, *chia chat* and *che chiat*. Step forward with the right leg and do a *sang kiao*, follow with a *sang kay*, and then a *hong ngan chiu*. Step into a *pi be*. Do a left hand *kay*, while the right hand executes a *kua*. Then execute a right hand *kay*, while the left hand executes a *kua*. Jump forward with the left leg into a *kut be*. Evade and execute a right *tioh* and then a left *tioh*. Rise up and do a right hand *chiat*. Drop again into a kneeling stance and do a *kwi kieng*. Rise up again a left hand *kim*. *Hua be* and right hand *puah*. Close. Stand in attention.

即束腰手，右手夾左肩，左手夾右肩。

This is also called **squeezing the waist hand** (*sok yiu chiu*). The right hand is tucked in at the left shoulder. The left hand is tucked in at the right shoulder.

練習法 - Training Method:

踏右足雙夾。退右足向右畔雙角節。並雙摔。退平向前雙角節。並雙摔。楊右足開綫。楊左足開綫。換右足雙撟中。掇節。駿斛。 換左足左手挑。換右足右手轉破。收立正。

Step forward with the right leg and execute the sang *kiap chiu*. Step back with the right leg and face right. Execute a *sang kak chat* and a *sang sut*. Step back and face the rear. Again do a *sang kak chat* and a *sang sut*. Step back with the right leg and face the left. Execute the *sang kak chat* and a *sang sut*. Step back and turn to the front and execute the *sang kak chat*. Follow with a *sang sut*. While doing a right *tap be*, execute a *sang kwi swa* and follow with a left *tap be* and *sang kwi swa*. Change to right leg lead and do a *sang kiao*. Follow with a *kak chat*, then a *tsun tow*. Change to left leg lead and execute a left *tioh*. Change to right leg and do a right *puah*. Close. Stand in attention.

雙開綫法 - Sang Kwi Suan Wat
DOUBLE OPEN LINE METHOD

從雙夾勢，開出左右平伸。

From the double tucked posture, open and extend both the left and the right hands.

練習法 - Training Method:

踏右足開綫。退右足向右向後向左向前雙開綫。踏右足蹕。並雙鉤。疊退雙橋。進左足蹕。退榻向右坐蓮。轉屈左手擋。呈身擒。進屈右手擋。呈身擒。換左足左手挑。換右足右手破。收立正。

Step forward with the right leg. Execute a *sang kwi suan*. Step back with the right leg, turning to the right side, the rear, the left side and the front. Execute a *sang kwi suan*. Step forward with a right *tat*. Follow this with a *sang kao*. Again step back and execute a *sang kiao*. Step forward and *tat* with the left leg. Cross the left leg behind the right and squat into a lotus position facing the right. Turn so that your right side faces the front. Turn and do a kneeling left hand *t'ng*. Rise up on the left hand *kim*. Step forward and do a kneeling right hand *t'ng*. Rise up on the right and do a *kim*. Change to left leg and execute a left *tioh*. Change to right leg and do a right *puah*. Close. Stand in attention.

封手拳法 - Hong Chiu Kun Wat
LOCKING HAND FIST METHOD

即獨參手，用左手封人右手節，右手擊之而捆下。

This is also called **single poison hand** (*dok cham chiu*). Use your left hand to immobilize your opponent's right elbow while your right hand strikes and entangles him.

練習法 - Training Method:

踏右足封機入。直進貫中拳。脫手雙豎拳。向左畔左手掀。提右足掃向後平馬右手開。左手開。踏左足左手掀。換右足右手掀。向右畔左手掀。提右足掃向前平馬右手開。左手開。踏左足左手挑。換右足右手轉破。收立正。

Step forward with the right leg. Execute the *hong chiu*. Step straight forward, do a *kwan tiong*. Release and do a *sang kia kun*. Turn toward your left and do a left *hian*. Lift the right leg and sweep to the rear and step into a left bow stance while doing a right hand *kai*. Then the left hand follows with a *kai*. Step with the left leg, left hand executes a *hian*. Shift to the right leg, right hand *hian*. Turn toward your right and do a left *hian*. Lift the right leg to sweep to the front and step into a right bow stance, and a right hand *kai*. Then the left hand *kai*. Change to left leg and execute a left *tioh*. Change to right leg and do a right *puah*. Close. Stand in attention.

平馬八字步。兩肘擊左右平伸。

In a horse stance, the two elbows shoot out to the sides.

練習法 - **Training Method:**

踏左足進平馬角節。並雙摔。疊退榻向前坐蓮。呈雙扭。右足蹾。左手切。右手釵。翻後左手擒。踏右足右手破。退榻向右坐蓮。轉屈左手擋。呈身擒。進屈右手擋。翻前屈左手擋。呈身擒。換右足右手破。收立正。

Step with the left leg into a horse stance. Execute a *sang kak chat*. Follow with a *sang sut*. Continue stepping back and squat into a lotus stance facing the front. Rise up and perform a *sang liu*. Execute a right *tat*. Follow with a left *chiat*. And a right *tueh*. Turn to the rear. Do a left hand *kim*. Step forward with the right leg, execute a right *pua*. Step back and squat into a lotus stance facing the right. Turn to a kneeling stance and execute a left hand *t'ng*. Rise up and left hand *kim*. Step forward into a kneeling stance and do a right hand *t'ng*. Turn to the front in a kneeling stance, left hand *t'ng*. Rist up and left hand *kim*. Change to right leg and do a right *puah*. Close. Stand in attention.

從角節或雙夾勢，用手背摔人面部。

From the **corner elbow** (*kak chiat*) or *double tucked-in* (*sang kiap*) posture, use the back of your hand to slap one's face.

練習法 - Training Method:

踏右足雙夾。並摔。退左足向左向後向右向前雙夾。並摔。進左足躂。並雙鉤。疊退雙撟。進右足躂。並雙鉤。直進打節。反墜。退右足左開右鞭。並左手挑。換右足右手破。收立正。

Step forward with the right foot and execute a *sang kiap* then immediately *sut*. Step back with the left foot to the left side, rear, right side and then front. Execute *sang kiap*, then *sut*. Step forward and execute a left *tat*. Follow with *sang kao*. Continue stepping back and do a *sang kiao*. Step forward and do a right *tat*. Follow with a *sang kao*. Step straight forward and do a *pa chat* then *sut*. Step back with the right leg and do a left *kai*, followed by a right *pian*. Follow with a left *tioh*. Change to right leg and do a right *puah*. Close. Stand in attention.

榻開弓法 - Tap Kwi Kieng Wat
OVERLAPPING OPEN BOW METHOD

提右足掃人前足於左畔，同時右手開弓勢。

Lift right leg and sweep the opponent's front leg toward the left side. Simultaneously, the right hand executes **pulling the bow posture** (*open bow chop*).

練習法 - Training Method:

疊進左足開弓。閃榻右足。開弓在馬。左轉向前開弓。進右足蹴。退右手切。並屈左手開弓。呈身擒。退左足屈右手開弓。呈身擒。換左手挑。換右手轉破。收立正。

Execute continuous stepping with the left foot and do a *kwi kieng*. Evade with a left *tap be po* and do a *kwi kieng*. Keep steady and turn left to face front while doing the *kwi kieng*. Step forward and execute a right *tat*. Bring the right leg back and execute a right *chiat*. Drop down into a *kut* and execute a left *kwi kieng*. Rise up and do a left *kim*. Step back with the left leg into a *kut* stance and execute a right *kwi kieng*. Rise up and do a right *kim*. Change to left leg and execute a left *tioh*. Change to right leg and do a right *puah*. Close. Stand in attention.

（增）齊眉手法 - Che Bi Chiu Wat
(EXTRA) - EYEBROW HAND METHOD

即參觀手,全身坐力在右足，左足起吊，同時左手開下，右手押上

This is also called *observing hand* (*cham guan chiu*). Put your weight on your right foot. Pull your left leg into a hanging stance. Simultaneously execute a left downward block, while the right hand covers up.

練習法 - Training Method:

閃右畔齊眉手。閃左畔齊眉手。進右屈雙摛。進左屈雙摛。呈身退左足右手擒。換左手擒。踏右足雙掛入。並扭。進左足蹮。並倒剪。反剪。鈎蹮。進屈撥。呈身扭。進抱牌。榻跳向後海底穿針。並倒剪。反剪。盤左轉翻後右手鞭。踏右足反搖。翻前踏右足撟。退馬屈。呈身擒。換右手轉破。收立正。

Evade to the right and execute the *che bi chiu*. Evade to the left and execute the *che bi chiu*. Step forward into right *kut* stance and execute a *sang li*. Step forward into a left *kut* stance and execute a *sang li*. Rise up and step the left leg back. The right hand executes a *kim*. Change to the left leg and left hand *kim*. Step forward with the right leg and do a *sang kwa lip*. Then follow with a *sang liu*. Step forward and kick with the left leg. Slide down to scissors position. Follow with a back scissors. Step forward into kneeling stance and execute a *so* grab. Rise up and execute a *liu*. Step forward and do a *po pai*. Overlap the legs and jump to the rear. Execute inserting needle beneath the sea. Follow with a scissors kick. Then do a reverse scissors kick. Roll toward the left as you face the rear. Do a right *pian*. Step forward and do a *wan be yao*. Step forward with the right foot and execute a *kiao*. Step back into a *kut* stance. Rise up and do a left *kim*. Change to right leg and do a right *puah*. Close. Stand in attention.

14 TEACHING ILLUSTRATION
教授圖式

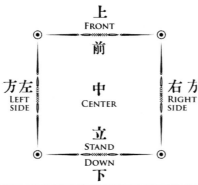

參觀人在上	Audience should be at the top
學生從下邊	Students should be at the lower section
排隊向看上	When you line up, face the audience
教員立左邊	Coach should stand at the left side
口令向看右	When you bark out the command, look to the right

15 TO LINE UP AND CALL OUT
排隊口令

立 – 正。向 (左) 右看 – 齊。向前 – 看。報數。稍息。立正。前行向前三步 – 走。雙數向前二步 – 走。稍 – 息。立 – 正。口令。第一節。預 – 備。(即請拳坐節)。起 – 數。(即動作之數)。停 – 止。(即收拳之雙曲手並垂下)。單數向前二步 – 走。後行向前三步 – 走。前行向後 – 轉。(即兩人對操法)。第一節。預 – 備。起 – 數。停 – 止。前行向後– 轉。口令。向(左)右 – 轉。左(右)轉彎。開步 – 走。或便步 – 走。左(右)轉 – 走。或踏脚 – 走。報數。立 – 正。散隊。至於排口。欲究其變法者。自有體操專書。可學而動作以算數練習可也。

Stand at attention and together face toward left or right and look forward. Call out, rest, stand at attention. First row take three steps forward. Even numbers take two steps, rest, stand at attention. Call out first section, get ready, fist salutation and sink the joints (*che chat*). This is one count followed by counting of movements. Stop. This is the closing fist. Odd numbers take three steps, first row turn toward the back. This is for two persons practice. First section, get ready, start counting, rest. First row turn back, call out, tun toward either right or left.Then start marching either straight or turn to left or right, follow and call out. Then dismiss and call out formation, you further refer to special manual and use them for this training.

Leonardo Co and Benito Tan

Volume 2

第二编

GENTLE ART TRAINING METHODS

柔術演習法 — 五章

16 | Fundamental Training and Corresponding Partner Training

（一）（二）柔術初步法 - 柔術頂機法

Editor's Note: *Volume 2 was written as five individual chapters: "Fundamental Training," "Corresponding Partner Training," Preparatory Fighting Training," "Nine Rotary Section Method," and "18 Scholars Method."*

Yu Chiok Sam described the partner exercises in two separate chapters. While this makes sense organizationally, it makes it difficult to employ this book as a learning manual. To help the reader see how the solo choreography of the drills comes together into partner drills, we have combined the "Fundamental Training" and "Corresponding Training" chapters into one chapter, placing together the corresponding exercise methods.

We also are not sure why Yu Chiok Sam included the liu or "sinking techniques of taking center line" in the solo execution of these exercises, but excluded the techniques from the parttner exercises. While we illustrated the exercises here as described by the author, we suggest you also do them with the inclusion of the liu movements. After all, taking control of the opponent's center is one of the primary strategies of Ngo Cho Kun.

The "five chapters" of exercise methods presented here, all derive from the form known as Ngo Ho Chien or "Five Tiger Battle" (五虎戰). This is the first form listed in Volume 3.

凡拳法欲演習者。如第一編之法。至於全體排隊者。可就立正。請拳。算數一。雙坐節。算數二。然後舉步至收拳。亦立正雙曲手。雙垂下。算數二。如動作算數。以十外者。殊與呼吸有碍。

Whenever the students are going to train, as in the first chapter, have them assemble in lines and stand at attention. On the first count, execute the salutation. On the second count, perform the double sinking wrist (*che chiat*). Then training starts and continues until the closing. After this, students should stand at attention with both hands cocked at their sides. This is one count. On the second count, drop the arms. If you are giving commands by the numbers, limit the counting to within 10 repetitions. Otherwise, the breathing of the students might be impaired.

The Opening Method
Do this opening for each of the five exercise sets.

拳手 - Kun Chiu
PUNCHING HAND

踏右足右手上拳。左手上拳。並扭。直進右手下拳。左手下拳。右手下拳。並扭。直退左手中拳。右手中拳。收立正。

Step forward with the right leg. Execute a right upper punch (*kun*). Follow this with a left upper punch (*kun*). Then wrench your fist (*liu*). Step straight forward. Execute a right lower punch (*kun*). Follow this with a left lower punch (*kun*). Then do a right lower punch (*kun*). Wrench your fist (*liu*). Step straight back. Do a left middle punch (*kun*) followed by a right middle punch (*kun*). Close. Stand Erect.

與拳手對操 - **Kup Kun Chiu Dui Chao**
PUNCHING HAND (OPPOSING SIDE)

踏右足右手擒。左手擒。直退右手開。左手開。右手開。直進左手鈎。右手鈎。收立正。

Step forward with the right leg. Grab (*kim*) with the right hand. Then grab (*kim*) with the left hand. Step straight back. Block down (*kai*) with the right hand. Then block down (*kai*) with the left hand. Block down again (*kai*) with the right hand. Step straight forward. Hook (*kao*) with the left hand. Then hook again (*kao*) with the right hand. Close. Stand erect.

KUN CHIU
PARTNER TRAINING DRILL

擒撞 - Kim Chieng
GRAB AND PUNCH

踏左足左手擒。右手一拳。退左足右手擒。左手一拳。進左足左手擒。右手一拳。收立正。

Step forward with the left leg. Grab (*kim*) with the left hand. Punch (*kun*) with the right hand. Step back with the left leg. Grab (*kim*) with the right hand. Punch (*kun*) with the left hand. Step forward with the left leg. Grab (*kim*) with the left hand. Punch (*kun*) with the right hand. Close. Stand erect.

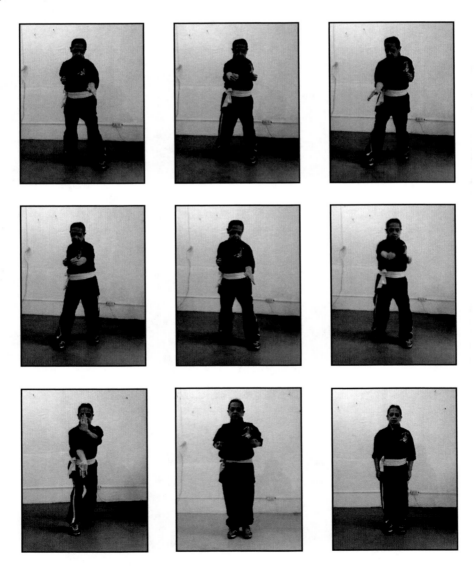

與擒撞對操 - Kup Kim Chieng Dui Chao
GRAB AND PUNCH (Opposing side)

踏左足左一拳。並右手開。進右足右一拳。並左手開。退左足左一拳。並右手開。收立正。

Step forward with the left leg. Punch (*kun*) with the left hand. Block down (*kai*) with the right hand. Step forward with the right leg. Punch (*kun*) with the right hand. Block down (*kai*) with the left hand. Step back with the left leg. Punch (*kun*) with the left hand. Block down (*kai*) with the right hand. Close. Stand Erect.

KIM CHIENG
PARTNER TRAINING DRILL

開切 - Kai Chiat
DOWNWARD BLOCK AND SLICE CHOP

踏左足左手開。右手切。退左足右手開。左手切。進左足左手開。右手切。收立正。

Step forward with the left leg. Execute a left downward block (*kai*). Slice chop (*chiat*) with the right hand. Step back with the left leg. Execute a right downward block (*kai*). Slice chop (*chiat*) with the left hand. Step forward with the left leg. Execute a left downward block (*kai*). Slice chop (*chiat*) with the right hand. Close. Stand erect.

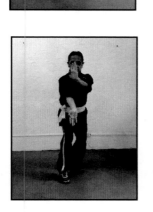

DOWNWARD BLOCK AND SLICE CHOP (OPPOSING SIDE)

踏左足左一拳。並右手擒。進右足右一拳。並左手擒。退左足左一拳。並右手擒。收立正。

Step forward with the left leg. Punch (*kun*) with the left hand. Grab (*kim*) with the right hand. Step forward with the right leg. Punch (*kun*) with the right hand. Grab (*kim*) with the left hand. Step back with the right leg. Punch (*kun*) with the left hand. Grab (*kim*) with the right hand. Close. Stand erect.

KAI CHIAT
PARTNER TRAINING DRILL

踏左足左手挑。右手截。退左足右手挑。左手截。進左足左手挑。右手截。收立正。

Step forward with the left leg. Execute a left flicking hand block (*tioh*). Intercept chop (*chà*) with the right hand. Step back with the left leg. Execute a right flicking hand block (*tioh*). Intercept chop (*chà*) with the left hand. Step forward with the left leg. Execute a left flicking hand block (*tioh*). Intercept chop (*chà*) with the right hand. Close. Stand erect.

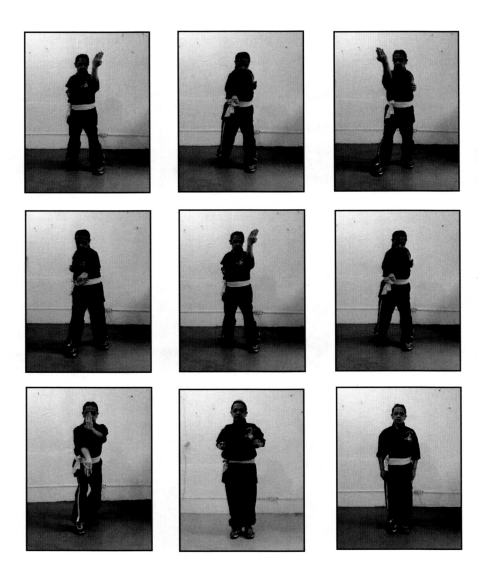

與挑截對操 - Kup Tioh Chà Dui Chao
FLICK AND INTERCEPT CHOP (OPPOSING SIDE)

踏左足左一擋。並右手盖。進右足右一擋。並左手盖。退左足左一擋。並右手盖。收立正。

Step forward with the left leg. Palm thrust (*t'ng*) with the left hand. Scoop block (*kay*) with the right hand. Step forward with the right leg. Palm thrust (*t'ng*) with the right hand. Scoop block (*kay*) with the left hand. Step back with the right leg. Palm thrust (*t'ng*) with the left hand. Scoop block (*kay*) with the right hand. Close. Stand erect.

TIOH CHÀ
PARTNER TRAINING DRILL

鈎搖 - Kao Yao
HOOK AND SHAKING STRIKE

踏左足角左鈎右搖。踏右足雙批中。並扭。右足躂。左手切。右手釟。收立正。

Step with the left leg to the left corner. Execute a left hook (*kao*). The right hand follows with a shaking strike (*yao*). Step forward into the center. Execute a double slap hand (*sang pueh*). Then wrench (*liu*) your fists. Kick (*tat*) with the right leg. Execute a left slice chop (*chiat*) and follow with a right side thrust (*tueh*). Close. Stand erect.

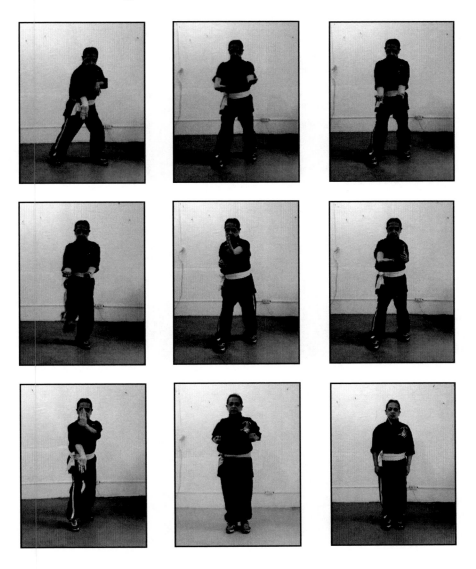

踏左足雙豎拳。退左足和手擒。並雙掛手。平馬右手搖。左手開。右手開。收立正。

Step forward with the left leg. Execute double vertical fist punch (*sang kia kun*). Step back with the left leg. Execute double grab (*ho chiu kim*). Follow with a double palm thrust (*sang kwa chiu*). Go into an even stance (*pieng ma*) and do a right shaking strike (*yao*). Follow with a left downward block (*kai*). Then follow again with a right downward block (*kai*).

KAO YAO
PARTNER TRAINING DRILL

Preparatory Fighting Drills

（三）准備對練法

Bonifacio Lim and Alexander Co

Editor's Note: *These five sections of Preparatory Fighting Drills are intended for intermediate Ngo Cho students. Beginners should first undergo proper training with Ngo Cho's two foundation forms: Sam Chien (labeled herein as Tit Be Chien) and Tien Te Lin Chien (labeled herein as Tien Li Chien). With diligent practice of these two foundation forms, beginners can temper their forearms, especially the bony section on the outer sides of the wrists—which are often referred to as "ngo ki."*

The first three sections of the Preparatory Fighting Drills are actually the Ngo Cho iron forearm training set called kong ngo ki, broken down into three sections. Constant practice and drilling of these three sections will lead to full tempering and strengthening of the iron forearms. In fact, Ngo Cho practitioners are known for their legendary forearm strength and the record now in China for the strongest iron forearm is held by a Ngo Cho practitioner.

The fourth and fifth sections of the Preparatory Fighting Drills serve as a two-man fighting set to familiarize students with close quarters and to develop enough confidence to fight in that range. The kut be (monkey jump, kneeling stance) trains students to move and weave in and out of attacking range. This set of training drills is actually an extracted version of the Ngo Cho Kun form called Se Mun Pa Kat ("Attacking the Four Directions").

雙對打 - Sang Dui Ta
DOUBLE STRIKING / FIGHTING

踏右足右手貢。踏左足左手貢。踏右足撟。踏左足撟。退右手貢。進左手貢。
退右手撟。退左手撟。進右手貢。換左手挑。換右手轉破。收立正。

Step forward with the right leg. Hammer strike (*kong*) with the right hand. Step forward with the left leg. Hammer strike (*kong*) with the left hand. Step forward with the right leg. Uppercut (*kiao*) with the right hand. Step forward with the left leg. Uppercut (*kiao*) with the left hand. Step back with the left leg. Hammer strike (*kong*) with the right hand. Step back with the right leg. Uppercut (*kiao*) with the right hand. Step back with the left leg. Uppercut (*kiao*) with the left hand. Step forward with the right leg. Hammer strike (*kong*) with the right hand. Shift to the left leg. Flick block (*tioh*) with the left hand. Shift to the right leg and do a rotating chop (*tsuan puah*) with the right hand. Close. Stand erect.

雙挑開 - Sang Tioh Kai
DOUBLE FLICK AND DOWNWARD BLOCK

踏右足右手挑。並開。換左足挑。並開。換右足開。並擒。直進翻後屈。呈身
擒。換右足挑。並開。換右足開。並擒。直進翻前屈。呈身擒。換右手轉破。
收立正。

Step forward with the right leg and flick blobk (*tioh*) with the right hand. Follow with
a downward block (*kai*). Change to the left leg and flick block (*tioh*) with the left hand.
Block down (*kai*) with the left hand. Follow with a grab (*kim*). Step straight forward and
turn to face the rear. Kneel (*kut*). Rise up and grab (*kim*) with the left. Shift to right leg
and flick block (*tioh*) with the right hand. Follow with a downward block (*kai*). Shift to left
leg and flick (*tioh*) with the left hand. Then block down (*kai*). Follow with a grab (*kim*).
Step straight forward and turn to face the front. Kneel (*kut*). Rise up and change to left leg.
Grab (*kim*) with the left hand. Shift to right leg and a rotating chop (*tsuan puah*) with the
right hand. Close. Stand erect.

雙挑屈 - Sang Tioh Kut
DOUBLE FLICK BLOCK AND KNEEL

踏右足右手挑。並屈。呈身擒。換左足左手挑。並屈。呈身擒。踏右足撟。退
右足屈。呈身擒。換右足開。並擒。翻後屈。呈身擒。踏右足撟。退馬屈。呈
身擒。換右足開。並擒。翻前屈。呈身擒。換右手轉破。收立正。

Step with the right leg. Flick block (*tioh*) with the right hand. Kneel (*kut*). Rise up and grab (*kim*) with your right. Change to left leg and flick block (*tioh*) with the left hand. Kneel (*kut*). Rise up and grab (*kim*) with the left hand. Step forward with the right leg. Execute a right uppercut (*kiao*). Step back with the right leg and kneel (*kut*). Rise up and grab (*kim*) with the left hand. Shift (*hua be*) to right leg and block down (*kai*) with the right hand. Then grab (*kim*) with the same hand. Turn toward the rear and kneel (*kut*). Rise up and grab (*kim*) with the left hand. Step forward with the right leg and do a right uppercut (*kiao*). Step back with the right leg and kneel (*kut*). Then rise up and grab (*kim*) with the left hand. Shift (*hua be*) to the right leg and block down (*kai*) with the right hand. Then grab (*kim*) with the same hand. Turn to the front and kneel (*kut*). Rise up and grab (*kim*) with the left hand. Shift (*hua be*) to the right leg and do a rotating chop (*tsuan puah*) with the right hand. Close. Stand erect.

踏右足右手擒。換左足左手擒。踏右足撟。退右足屈。呈身擒。換右足挑。
屈。擒。翻後屈。呈身擒。踏右足撟。退右足屈。呈身擒。換右足挑。屈。
擒。翻前屈。呈身擒。換右手轉破。收立正。

Step with the right leg and grab (*kim*) with the right. Shift (*hua be*) to the left leg and grab (*kim*) with the left hand. Step forward with the right leg. Execute a right uppercut (*kiao*). Step back with the right leg and kneel (*kut*). Rise up and grab (*kim*) with the left hand. Shift (*hua be*) to right leg and flick block (*tioh*) with the right hand. Kneel (*kut*) and grab (*kim*) with the right hand. Turn to face the rear and kneel (*kut*). Rise up and grab (*kim*) with the left hand. Shift (*hua be*) to the right leg and flick block (*tioh*) with the right hand. Kneel (*kut*) and grab (*kim*) with the right hand. Turn to face the front and kneel (*kut*). Rise up and grab (*kim*) with the left hand. Shift (*hua be*) to right leg and do a right rotating chop (*tsuan puah*). Close. Stand erect.

與雙擒屈對操 - Kup Sang Kim Kut Dui Tsao
DOUBLE KNEELING GRAB (Opposing Side)

踏右足右手一拳。換左足左手一拳。退右手搖。進左足蹻。右手一拳。退右手
掀。右足蹻。右手一拳。翻後左足蹻。右手一拳。退右手搖。進左足蹻。右手
一拳。退右手掀。右足蹻。右手一拳。翻前左足蹻。右手一拳。退右手轉破。
收立正。

Step with the right leg. Punch (*kun*) with the right hand. Shift to left leg and punch (*kun*) with the left hand. Step back with the right leg and shake (*yao*) with the right hand. Step forward and kick (*tat*) with the left leg. Punch (*kun*) with the right hand. Step back with the right leg and do a right turning block (*hian*). Kick (*tat*) with the right leg. Punch (*kun*) with the right hand. Turn to face the rear and kick (*tat*) with the left leg. Punch (*kun*) with the right hand. Step back with the right leg. Shake (*yao*) with the right hand. Step forward with the left and kick (*tat*). Punch (*kun*) with the right hand. Step back with the right leg and do a right turning block (*hian*). Kick (*tat*) with the right leg and punch (*kun*) with the right hand. Turn to face the front. Kick (*tat*) with the left hand and punch (*kun*) with the right hand. Step back with the right leg and do a rotating chop (*tsuan puah*). Close. Stand erect.

Ediotr's Note: *The Nine Section Rotary Method is a set of nine individual training drills. Unlike the 18 Scholars, which are more comprehensive drills covering the basic to advanced techniques, the Nine Rotaries concentrate on advanced movements and techniques. The reason for the emergence of the Nine Rotaries in the training is to make it easier for the Ngo Cho Kun practitioners to remember the important or salient points of the system, given that Ngo Cho Kun has nearly four-dozen standard solo, empty-hand forms (not including special froms and two-man forms). Because it is seemingly impossible for students to master all of the forms, in the Asian tradition of kung-fu learning, not all of the forms are taught to all students. Normally, everyone learns the basic forms but the advanced ones are selectively taught to a student based on their individual physique, skills, interest and attitude. The Nine Rotaries are comprised of key drills extracting the essential aspects of each important form for a sort of "crash course" in techniques. The practitioner can freely interchange or "rotate" these nine drills to create combined or varied drills for deeper training.*

Pictorial Overview of the Nine Section Rotary Methods

孩兒跳 - **Hi Li Tiao**
JUMPING CHILD

踏左足雙鈎。換右足雙貢。跳進左足右轉翻後抱牌。再跳進翻前抱牌。踏左足開弓。閃角右手貢。踏右足右手開。換左足左手挑。退右足右手轉破。收立正。

Stand with the left leg forward and execute a double hook block (*sang kao*). Shift to the right leg and execute a double hammer strike (*sang kong*). Jump forward with the left leg crossing to the right corner so that you turn and face the rear. Execute the holding the tablet strike (*po pai*). Again jump and turn to the front. Execute a holding the tablet strike (*po pai*). Step forward with the left leg and do an open bow chop (*kwi kieng*). Evade to the corner and do a right hammer strike (*kong*). Step forward with the right leg and execute a right downward block (*kai*). Shift to the left leg and execute a left flicking block (*tioh*). Shift to the right leg and do a rotating chop (*tsuan puah*) with the right hand. Close. Stand erect.

雙龍鳳 - Sang Lien Hong
DOUBLE DRAGON PHOENIX

踏右足雙擋。並扭。退右足向後雙開綫。再退右足向前雙開綫。直進右手啄。
並盖。左手鞭。換左足左手啄。並盖。右手鞭。退左足右手擒。左手擒。直進
右一拳。收立正。

Step with the right leg and execute a double palm thrust (*sang t'ng*), followed by a wrench (*liu*). Step back with right leg and face toward the rear and execute double openline block (*sang kwi sua*). Step back again with the right leg and face the front. Execute a double open line block (*sang kwi sua*). Step forward with the right leg and do a finger thrust (*tok*) with the right hand. Then execute a scoop block (*kay*). Follow with a left backfist (*pian*). Shift to the left leg and finger thrust (*tok*) with the left hand. Then execute a scoop block (*kay*). Follow with a right backfist (*pian*). Step back with the left leg and grab (*kim*) with the right hand. Then grab (*kim*) with the left hand. Step straight forward and punch (*kun*) with the right hand. Close. Stand erect.

三跳澗 - Sang Tiao Gan
JUMPING THREE CANALS

踏左足左手擒。右手切。換右足右手擒。左手切。退右足左手盖。右切。左切。踏右足雙掛入。直進雙擋。並扭。跳退抱牌。疊進右足蹖。並雙鈎。疊退寄右足雙撟。雙盖。雙鳳眼手。收立正。

Step forward with the left leg and grab (*kim*) with the left hand. Slice chop (*chiat*) with the right hand. Shift to right leg. Grab (*kim*) with the right hand and slice chop (*chiat*) with the left hand. Step back with the right leg and scoop block (*kay*) with the left hand. Follow this with a right hand slice chop (*chiat*) and a left hand slice chop (*chiat*). Step forward with the right leg and do a double palm thrust (*sang kwa lip*). Follow with a straight forward double palm thrust (*sang t'ng*) and a double wrench (*sang liu*). Jump back while executing a holding the tablet strike (*po pai*). Execute a continuous step (*tiap chin*) to the front and kick (*tat*) with the right leg. Then do a double hook block (*sang kao*). Execute a continuous step backward and go into a right hanging leg stance (*king tzi be*). Do a double uppercut (*sang kiao*). Follow with double scoop block (*sang kay*). Then follow with a double phoenix-eye hand (*sang hong ngan chiu*). Close. Stand erect.

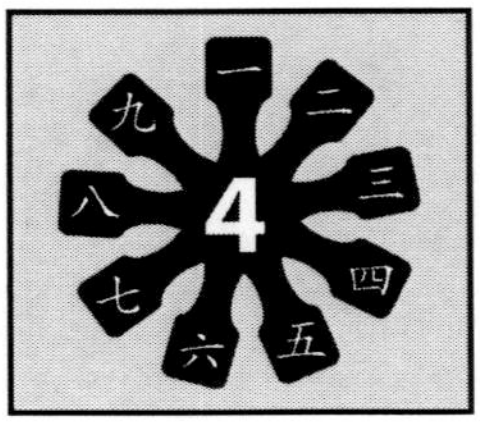

回馬鞭 - Way Ma Pien
RETURNING BACKFIST

踏左角左手鈎。右手搖。踏右足雙批。旋螺跳向前右手鞭。平馬右鈎左搖。踏左足雙批。換右足雙批。並扭。右足躂。左手切。右手釵。收立正。

Step to the left corner and hook (*kao*) with the left hand hand while executing a shaking strike (*yao*) with the right hand. Step forward with the right leg and do a double slap hand (*sang pueh*). Jump and spin forward while executing a right backfist (*pian*). Go into a right bow stance (*kia ka be*) and hook *(kao)* with the right hand while the left hand executes a shaking strike (*yao*). Step forward with the left leg and do a double slap hand (*sang pueh*), followed by a double wrench (*sang liu*). Kick (*tat*) with the right leg. Slice chop (*chiat*) with the left hand and side chop (*tueh*) with the right hand. Close. Stand erect.

雙疪肩 - Sang Tiao Kian
DOUBLE SIDE SHOULDER (THRUST)

平馬閃左畔右手疪肩。閃右畔左手疪肩。再閃右手疪肩。再閃左手疪肩。平馬
右手開。左手開。踏左足左手挑。換右足右手轉破。收立正。

Evade to the left side in an even stance (*pieng ma*). Execute a right side shoulder thrust (*tiao kian*). Evade toward the right. Execute a left side shoulder thrust (*tiao kian*). Again, evade to the left. Execute a right side shoulder thrust (*tiao kian*). Again, evade to the right. Execute a left side shoulder thrust (*tiao kian*). Shift to a horse stance (*chien be*) while performing a downward block (*kai*) with the right hand. Follow with a left hand downward block (*kai*). Step with the left leg and do a flick block (*tioh*) with the left hand. Shift to the right leg and do a rotating chop (*tsuan puah*) with the right hand. Close. Stand erect.

鐵槌沉 - Tie Tui Tim
METAL HAMMER SINKING

踏右足右手鞭。換左足左手開。換右足右手貢。換左足左手擒。換右足右手沉。閃角右擒。左搖。換左足左手擒。右搖。踏右足雙捲手。直進雙彈。退寄右手挑。左手挑。右手釵。收立正。

Step forward with the right leg and execute a right backfist (*pian*). Shift to the left leg and block down (*kai*) with the left hand. Shift to right leg and hammer strike (*kong*) with the right hand. Shift to the left leg and grab (*kim*) with the left hand. Shift to the right leg and execute sinking hand (*tim chiu*) with the right hand. Evade to the corner and grab (*kim*) with the right hand while executing a shaking strike (*yao*) with the left hand. Shift to the left leg and grab (*kim*) with the left hand while executing a shaking strike (*yao*) with the right hand. Step forward with the right leg and do double coiling hand grab (*sang k'ng chiu*). Step straight forward and execute a double spring hand chop (*sang tua*). Step back into a right hanging leg stance (*tiao be*) and flick block (*tioh*) with the right hand. Flick block (*tioh*) with the left and side thrust (*tueh*) with the right. Close. Stand erect.

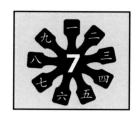

抄鞭法 - Sha Pien Wat
GRASP AND WHIP METHOD

踏左足左手抄右手鞭。踏右足右手反馬搖。翻後踏右足右手撟。翻前屈開弓。
呈身左擒。踏右足右手貢。並掀。左手切。右手釵。收立正。

Step to the left corner. Grasp (*sha*) with the left hand and execute a backfist (*pian*) with the right hand. Step forward with the right leg and do a reverse shaking strike (*wan be yao*). Turn to face the rear. Step forward with the right leg and do a right uppercut (*kiao*). Turn to face the front and kneel (*kut*) with an open bow chop (*kwi kieng*). Rise up and grab (*kim*) with the left hand. Step forward with the right leg and hammer strike (*kong*) with the right hand. Follow with a turning block (*hian*). Then slice chop (*chiat*) with the left hand and side thrust (*tueh*) with the right hand. Close. Stand erect.

雙坐蓮 - Sang Che Lien
DOUBLE SITTING LOTUS

踏左足左手擒。平馬右手擒。閃屈左。呈身雙捲手。右足躂。平馬左手擒。閃
屈右。呈身左手擒。右手刈。跳進屈指地。呈身雙挑。進左屈雙擒。進右屈雙
擒。呈身退右足左手擒。踏右足右手破。疊退榻向右坐蓮。呈轉向前力士擋。
並擒。踏右足雙掛入。疊退榻向中坐蓮。呈身雙擒。並扭。右足躂。左手切。
右手釗。收立正。

Step forward with the left leg and grab (*kim*) with the left hand. Shift to a left bow stance
(*kieng tzi be*) and evade to the left and kneel (*kut*). Grab (*kim*) with the right hand. Rise
up and execute double curling grab hold (*sang k'ng chiu*). Kick (*tat*) with the right leg and
land in a right bow stance (*king tzi be*). Grab (*kim*) with the left hand while evading to the
right and kneeling (*kut*). Rise up and grab (*kim*) with the left hand while slashing (*kwa*)
with the right hand. Jump forward and kneel (*chi teh kut*). Rise up and do a double flick
block (*sang tioh*). Step forward and kneel (*kut*) on the left knee. Execute double splitting
hand block (*sang li*). Step forward and kneel (*kut*) on the right knee. Execute double splitting hand block (*sang li*). Rise up, step back with the right leg and grab (*kim*) with the left
hand. Step forward with the right leg and chop (*puah*) with the right hand. Execute con-
tinuouse stepping to the rear (*tiap teh*) and sit in lotus posture (*che lien kut*) facing right.
Twist toward the front and do a strong man thrust (*liak si t'ng*). Then grab (*kim*) with the
left hand. Step forward with the right leg and execute a double palm thrust (*sang kwa lip*).
Execute continuous stepping to the rear (*tiap teh*) and sit in the lotus position (*che lien kut*)
facing the front. Rise up and double grab (*sang kim*), then double wrench (*sang liu*). Kick
(*tat*) with the right leg. Plant the foot and slice chop (*chiat*) with the left hand then side
thrust (*tueh*) with the right hand. Close. Stand erect.

雙挼法 - Sang So Wat
DOUBLE GRABBING HOLD METHOD

踏右角雙挼。踏左角雙挼。踏右角雙捲中。進抱牌。榻馬向後海底針。提右足倒左側盤剪。翻左轉向後左抄右鞭。踏右足反馬搖。翻前踏右足右手撟。翻後屈左手開。呈身擒。踏右足雙掛入。翻前左手開。踏右足屈右手擋。呈身擒。換左手挑。換右手轉破。收立正。

Step to the right corner and do double grabbing hold (*sang so*). Step to the left corner and do double grabbing hold (*sang so*). Step to the center and do double curling grab hold (*sang k'ng chiu*). Step forward and execute the holding the tablet strike (*po pai*). Turn to the rear while doing an overlapping step (*tap be po*) to slide down into the sea bottom piercing needle technique (*hai twe cham*). Fall to your left and raise the right leg in order to execute a scissors maneuver (*pwan chian*). Turn toward your left and face the rear. Execute a left grasping right backfist (*sha pian*). Step forward with the right leg and execute a reverse shaking strike (*wan be yao*). Turn to the front, stepping forward with the right leg, uppercut (*kiao*) with the right hand. Turn toward the rear as you kneel (*kut*) and block down (*kai*) with the left hand. Rise up and grab (*kim*) with the left hand. Step forward with the right leg and do a double palm thrust (*sang kwa lip*). Turn to the front and block down (*kai*) with the left hand. Kneel (*kut*) forward with the right leg and palm thrust (*t'ng*) with the right hand. Rise up and grab (*kim*) with the right hand. Shift to the left leg and flick block (*tioh*) with the left hand. Shift to the right leg and do a rotating chop (*tsuan puah*) with the right hand. Close. Stand erect.

19 EIGHTEEN SCHOLARS METHOD
十八學士法

Editor's Note: As the name implies, the 18 Scholars Method is a collection of 18 different, important and tediously developed training drills. According to the late grandmaster, Tan Ka Hong, the 18 Scholars can be thought of as "advanced degree" training in Ngo Cho Kun. Meaning that it is a composite study of the important techniques from very basic blocks to advanced strikes and counters. These 18 sections of techniques consist of concise training drills, and within these 18 sections are extracted the very foundation form of Tien Ti Lin Chien ("Heavan, Earth and Man Battle") for training ngo ki lat ("five limb power"), to the combination of defensive and offencive techniques, like: kim chieng (grab and punch), tio cha (outside block intercepting chop), kai chat (low block and chop), kao yao (hook and attack); to offense techniques like the lohan chiu (arhat hand), kiap sut (backhand strike), and kao chien (scissors leg). Constant training of the 18 Scholars Method will prepare students for the wide variety of Ngo Cho Kun offensive and defensive fighting techniques.

"An Elegant Party," shows a banquet hosted by the emperor for scholar-officials. Song Dynasty.

踏左足左手擒。右手一拳。退左足右手擒。左手一拳。進左足左手擒。右手一拳。踏右足右手擒。左手一拳。退右足左手擒。右手一拳。進右足右手擒。左手一拳。右手一拳。收立正。

Step forward with the left leg and grab (*kim*) with the left hand. Punch (*kun*) with the right hand. Step back with the left leg and grab (*kim*) with the right hand. Punch (*kun*) with the left hand. Step forward with the left leg and grab (*kim*) with the left hand. Punch (*kun*) with the right hand. Step forward with the right leg and grab (*kim*) with the right hand. Punch (*kun*) with the left hand. Step back with the right leg and grab (*kim*) with the left hand. Punch (*kun*) with the right hand. Step forward with the right leg and grab (*kim*) with the right hand. Punch (*kun*) with the left hand. Punch (*kun*) with the right hand. Close. Stand erect.

前後開切
FRONT / BACK DOWNWARD BLOCK AND SLICE CHOP

踏左足左手開。右手切。踏右足右手開。左手切。踏左足左手開。右手切。翻後右手開。左手切。踏左足左手開。右手切。踏右足右手開。左手切。翻前左手開。右手切。換右足右手開。左手切。右手釵。收立正。

Step forward with the left leg and block down (*kai*) with the left hand. Slice chop (*chiat*) with the right hand. Step forward with the right leg and block down (*kai*) with the right hand. Slice chop (*chiat*) with the left hand. Step forward with the left leg and block down (*kai*) with the left hand. Slice chop (*chiat*) with the right hand. Turn to the rear and block down (*kai*) with the right hand. Slice chop (*chiat*) with the left hand. Step forward with the left leg and block down (*kai*) with the left hand. Slice chop (*chiat*) with the right hand. Step forward with the right leg and block down (*kai*) with the right hand. Slice chop (*chiat*) with the left hand. Turn to the front and block down (*kai*) with the left hand. Slice chop (*chiat*) with the right hand. Shift to the right leg and block down (*kai*) with the right hand. Slice chop (*chiat*) with the left hand. Side thrust (*tueh*) with the right hand. Close. Stand erect.

左右鈎搖
LEFT RIGHT HOOK AND SHAKE

踏左角左手鈎。右手搖。踏右角右手鈎。左手搖。踏中左手鈎。右手搖。換右足雙批。換左足雙批。換右足雙批。並扭。右足蹬。左手切。右手釗。收立正。

Step to the left corner. Hook (*kao*) with the left hand. Do a shaking strike (*yao*) with the right hand. Step to the right corner. Hook (*kao*) with the right hand. Do a shaking strike (*yao*) with the right hand. Step to the center. Hook (*kao*) with the left hand. Do a shaking strike (*yao*) with the right hand. Shift to the right and execute a double slap (*sang pueh*). Shift to the left and execute a double slap (*sang pueh*). Shift to the right and execute a double slap (*sang pueh*). Then wrench (*liu*). Kick (*tat*) with the right foot. Slice chop (*chiat*) with the left hand. Side thrust (*tueh*) with the right hand. Close. Stand erect.

四門挑
FOUR GATES FLICKING BLOCK

踏右足右手挑。左手截。翻後左手挑。右手截。翻前右手開。左手切。向左畔
左手開。右手切。向右畔右手開。左手切。向前左手挑。換右足右手轉破。收
立正。

Step forward with the right leg and flick block (*tioh*) with the right hand. Intercept chop (*cha*) with the left hand. Turn to the rear and flick block (*tioh*) with the left hand. Intercept chop (*cha*) with the right hand. Turn to the front and block down (*kai*) with the right hand. Slice chop (*chiat*) with the left hand. Turn to face the left and block down (*kai*) with the left hand. Slice chop (*chiat*) with the right hand. Turn to face the right and block down (*kai*) with the right hand. Slice chop (*chiat*) with the left hand. Turn to face the front and flick block (*tioh*) with the left hand. Shift to the right leg and do a rotating chop (*tsuan puah*) with the right hand. Close. Stand erect.

五步擒
FIVE STEP GRAB

向左角左手擒。向右角右手擒。向前左手擒。換右足右手擒。換左足左手擒。
右手一拳。左手一拳。並扭。踏右足右手一拳。左手一拳。右手一拳。退寄雙
破。進榻雙攦。翻後左手開。踏右足右手釵。翻前雙搖。退寄左足雙鈎。踏右
足躂。左手切。右手釵。收立正。

Face the left corner and grab (*kim*) with the left hand. Face the right corner and grab (*kim*) with the right hand. Face the front and grab (*kim*) with the left hand. Shift to the right leg and grab (*kim*) with the right hand. Shift to the left leg and grab (*kim*) with the left hand. Punch (*kun*) with the right hand. Then punch (*kun*) with the left hand. Follow with a wrench (*liu*). Step forward with the right foot and punch (*kun*) with the right hand, then the left hand, then the right hand. Step back into a hanging leg stance (*kia ka*) and do double downward chop (*sang puah*). Step forward with an overlapping step (*tap be po*) and execute a double split (*sang li*). Turn to face the rear and block down (*kai*) with the left hand. Step forward with the right leg and do a right side thrust (*tueh*). Turn to face the front and execute a double shaking strike (*sang yao*). Step back into a left hanging leg stance (*kia ka be*) and do a double hook (*sang ka*). Step forward and kick (*tat*) with the right leg and slice chop (*chiat*) with the left hand. Side thrust (*tueh*) with the right hand. Close. Stand erect.

三進退
THREE ADVANCE / RETREAT

踏右足雙陰插。扭雙墜。雙挑。坐節。吞手。駿手。直馬三進三退如法。收立正。

Step forward with the right leg and execute double horizontal finger thrust (*sang yim cha*), then wrench (*liu*). Execute double falling punch (*sang tui kun*). Follow with a double flicking block (*sang tioh*), then sink the wrists (*che chat*). Execute double swallowing hand (*tun chiu*). Then perform vibrating hand (*tsun tao*). Step straight forward three times and backward three times while executing the same sequence. Close. Stand erect.

Editor's Note: These are the primary movements of the form called "Tien Ti Lin Chien" or "Heaven Shape Battle" (天字戰), more commonly known as "Heaven, Earth, Man Battle."

踏左足左手擒。踏右足雙關。退寄雙鈎。進打節。右手開。左手切。右手釵。翻後至前如法。收立正。

Step forward with the left leg and grab (*kim*) with the left hand. Step forward with the right leg and do double closing scissors (*sang kwi chian*). Step back into hanging leg (*kia ka*) and double hook (*sang kao*). Step forward and do an elbow strike (*pa chat*). Block down (*kai*) with the right hand. Slice chop (*chiat*) with the left hand. Then side thrust (*tueh*) with the right hand. Turn to the rear and perform the same sequence. Then perform it once more to the front. Close. Stand erect.

Editor's Note: *This is the closing sequence of the forms "Sam Chien" (Three Battles) (三戰) and "Tien Ti Lin Chien" (Heavan, Earth and Man Battle) (天字戰).*

鳳尾彩
ELEGANT PHOENIX TAIL

走馬向右角雙掹。向左角雙掹。踏右足向中鳳尾彩。扭進雙陰插。再扭。雙鈎入。駿肚出。退右足左手擒。換右足鐵槌沉江。退寄和手擒。左手切。右鳳眼。收立正。

Walk toward the right corner and do double grabbing hold (*sang so*). Face the left corner and do double grabbing hold (*sang so*). Step with the right leg to the center and do elegant phoenix tail hand (*hong be tsai*), the wrench (*liu*). Perform double horizontal finger thrust (*sang yim cha*), wrench (*liu*). Perform double hooking inward (*sang kao lip*). Follow with double vibrating hand (*tsun tao chut*) while pushing out. Step back with the right leg and grab (*kim*) with the left hand. Shift to the right leg and do a right hammer sinking in the river fist (*ti twi tim kang*). Step back into a hanging leg (*kia ka*) and do double hand grab (*ho chiu kim*). Slice chop (*chiat*) with the left hand. Do a right phoenix eye (*hong ngan*). Close. Stand erect.

獨步立
SINGLE STANDING STEP

踏右足雙陰插。扭雙墜。雙挑。坐節。退寄雙鈎。進雙撟。掇節。駿肚。直進退如法。收立正。

Step forward with the right leg and execute a double horizontal finger thrust (*sang yim cha*), wrench (*liu*). Perform a double falling punch (*sang twi*). Follow with a double flicking block (*sang tioh*). Sink the wrists (*che chat*). Step back into hanging leg (*kia ka*) and double hook (sang kao). Step forward and double uppercut (*sang kiao*). Then execute double plucking elbow (*sang kwa chat*). Follow with vibrating hand (*tsun chiu*). Step straight forward and backward, repeating the sequence. Close. Stand erect.

Editor's Note: *This is the beginning sequence of the form "Lieng Tao Chien" (Dragon Head Battle)* (龍頭戰).

龍吐珠
DRAGON SPITTING PEARL

踏左足左手啄。並盖。右手鞭。換右足右手啄。並盖。左手鞭。換左足左手啄。並盖。右手鞭。退左足雙批。換左足雙批。向右畔右手擒。左手一拳。右手一拳。左手一拳。翻左畔左手擒。右手一拳。左手一拳。右手一拳。向前右手擒。並左手擒。右手一拳。收立正。

Step forward with the left leg. Finger thrust (*tok*) with the left hand. Follow with a scoop block (*kay*), and then a right backfist (*pian*). Switch to the right leg and finger thrust (*tok*) with the right hand. Follow with a scoop block (*kay*). And then a left backfist (*pian*). Switch to the left leg and finger thrust (*tok*) with the left hand. Follow with a scoop block (*kay*). And then a right backfist (*pian*). Step back with the left leg and do a double slap hand (*sang pueh*). Shift to the left leg and do double slap hand (*sang pueh*). Turn to face the right and grab (*kim*) with the right hand, punch (*kun*) with the left hand, punch (*kun*) with the right hand, punch (*kun*) with the left hand. Turn to face the left side and grab (*kim*) with the left hand, punch (*kun*) with the right hand, punch (*kun*) with the left hand, punch (*kun*) with the right hand. Face the front and grab (*kim*) with the right hand. Then grab (*kim*) with the left hand. Punch (*kun*) with the right hand. Close. Stand erect.

Editor's Note: *This is nearly identical to the second half of the form "Lieng Tao Chien" (Dragon Head Battle) (龍頭戰).*

雙駿躂
DOUBLE VIBRATING KICK

踏右足雙擋。並扭。退右足抱盤挨。提右足駿躂右畔。翻左畔左手盖。提左足
駿躂。向前右手開。換左足左手開。並擒。換右足打節。反墜。退右足右手
擋。並擒。踏右足雙扯剪。並右挑。左切。翻後左手擒。踏右足雙扯剪。並右
挑。左切。翻前左手擒。踏右足加刀剪。退寄雙鈎。右足躂。左手切。右手
釵。收立正。

Step forward with the right leg and double palm thrust (*sang t'ng*). Then wrench (*liu*). Step
back with the right leg and do holding the tray grab (*po pua so*). Raise the right leg and kick
(*tat*) to the right. Turn to face the left and scoop block (*kay*) with the left hand. Raise the
left leg and kick (*tat*) to the left. Face forward and block down (*kai*) with the right hand.
Shift to the left leg and block down (*kai*) with the left hand. Follow with a grab (*kim*). Shift
to the right leg and do an elbow strike (*pa chat*) and a backfist (*wan tui*). Step back with the
right leg and palm thrust (*t'ng*) with the right hand. Follow with a grab (*kim*). Step forward
with the right leg and do double clip scissors (*sang chi chian*). Then execute right flicking
block (*tioh*) and a left slice chop (*chiat*). Turn to the rear and grab (*kim*) with the left hand.
Step forward with the right foot and do double clip scissors (*sang chi chian*). Then execute
a right flicking block (*tioh*) and a left slice chop (*chiat*). Turn to the front and grab (*kim*)
with the left hand. Step forward with the righ foot and perform scissor cutting hand (*ka
to chian*). Step back into a hanging leg stance (*kai ka*) while executing double hook (*sang
kao*). Kick (*tat*) with the right leg. Slice chop (*chiat*) with the left hand. Side thrust (*tueh*)
with the right hand. Close. Stand erect.

雙摽插
DOUBLE THROWING THRUST

退左足平馬右手直插。左手直插。退左足右手摽插。退右足左手摽插。退左足
閃向左雙墜。向前雙串拳。平馬右手盖。並一拳。退右足閃向右雙墜。向前雙
串拳。平馬左手盖。並一拳。踏右足抱盤梭。並雙彈。退寄右手挑。左手挑。
直進右手釵。收立正。

Step back with the left leg into an even stance (*pieng ma*). Execute a right hand straight finger thrust (*tit cha*). And then a left hand straight finger thrust (*tit cha*). Step back with the left leg and perform throwing thrust (*pio cha*) with the right hand. Step back with the right leg and perform throwing thrust (*pio cha*) with the left hand. Step back with the left leg while simultaneously evading and turning to the left. Execute double falling punch (*sang tui*). Face the front and perform double piercing fist (*sang ch'ng kun*). Go into a level horse stance and scoop block (*kay*) with the right hand. Follow with a punch (*kun*). Step back with the right leg while evading and turning to the right. Execute double falling punch (*sang tui*). Face the front and perform double piercing fist (*sang ch'ng kun*). Go into a level horse stance (*pieng ma*) and scoop block (*kay*) with the left hand. Follow with a punch (*kun*). Step forward with the right leg and execute holding the tray grab (*po pua so*). Immediately follow with a double spring chop (*sang tua*). Step back into a hanging leg stance (*kia ka*) and flick block (*tioh*) with the right hand. Flick block (*tioh*) with the left hand. Step straight forward with the right leg and do a side thrust (*tueh*) with the right hand. Close. Stand erect.

Editor's Note: *This is nearly identical to the end of the form "Sam Chien Sip Li" (Three Battle Cross Pattern) (*十字戰*).*

<table>
<tr><td>

雙擒榻
DOUBLE SPLITTING & OVERLAPPING

</td><td>

</td></tr>
</table>

閃榻向左雙擒。閃榻向右雙擒。再閃左雙擒。再閃右雙擒。踏左足左手挑。並屈開。呈身擒。踏右足右手挑。並屈開。呈身擒。換左足左手挑。換右足右手轉破。收立正。

Execute an overlapping step (*tap be*) to the left and do a double split (*sang li*). Evade to the right and do a double split (*sang li*). Then evade to the left and again do a double split (*sang li*). Follow with a right double split (*sang li*). Step forward with the left leg and flick block (*tioh*) with the left hand. Immediately kneel (*kut*) and block down (*kai*). Rise up and grab (*kim*) with the left hand. Step forward with the right leg and flick block (*tioh*) with the right hand. Immediately kneel (*kut*) and block down (*kai*). Rise up and grab (*kim*) with the right hand. Shift to the left leg and flick (tioh) with the left hand. Shift to the right leg and perform a rotating chop (*tsuan puah*) with the right hand. Close. Stand erect.

雙開弓
DOUBLE OPEN BOW

踏左足雙鈎。扯進右足蹕。並雙彈。退右足向後右手開弓。在馬向前左手開弓。並擒。踏右足打節。進抱牌。退右足左鈎右搖。退左足右鈎左搖。疊進右足雙掛入。退右足抱盤撥。退左足抱盤撥。直進抱牌。進左足蹕。並雙開。換右足雙貢。直進右手掀。左手切。退右足左手挑。換右足右手轉破。收立正。

Step forward with the left leg and do double hook (*sang kao*). Kick (*tat*) with the right leg. Immediately perform double spring chop (*sang tua*). Step back with the right leg to face the rear and execute an open bow chop (*kwi kieng*) with the right hand. In the same stance, turn to face the front and execute a left open bow chop (*kwi kieng*). Then grab (*kim*) with the same hand. Step forward with the right leg and execute an elbow strike (*pa chat*). Step forward executing holding the tablet (*po pai*). Step back with the right leg and hook (*kao*) with the left hand while executing a shaking strike (*yao*) with the right hand. Step back with the left leg and hook (*kao*) with the right hand while executing a shaking strike (*yao*) with the left hand. Do continuous stepping forward with the right leg and execute the double hanging palms (*sang kwa lip*). Step back with the right leg and do a holding the tray grab (*po pua so*). Step back with the left leg and do a holding the tray grab (*po pua so*). Step straight forward executing holding the tablet strike (*po pai*). Kick (*tat*) with the right leg. Then immediately perform a double downward block (*sang kai*). Shift to the right leg and perform double hammer (*sang kong*). Step straight forward, executing a right turning block (*hian*). Slice chop (*chiat*) with the left hand. Step back with the right leg and flick block (*tioh*) with the left hand. Shift to the right leg and perform a rotating chop (*tsuan puah*) with the right hand. Close. Stand erect.

雙夾法
DOUBLE CLIP METHOD

疊進右足雙夾。退右足向右畔雙角節。並摔。退換平馬向前雙角節。並摔。退榻立中雙開綫。疊進左足雙撟。退左足雙鈎。退右足雙按手。閃左畔齊眉手。閃右畔齊眉手。進左足左手挑中。換右足右手轉破。收立正。

Execute continuous stepping with the right leg and do a double clip (*sang kiap*). Step back with the right leg and face the right. Do a double corner elbow (*sang kak chat*). Immediately follow with a back hand slap (*sut*). Step back and shift into a horse stance facing the front. Do a double corner elbow (*sang kak chat*). Immediately follow with a back hand slap (*sut*). Step back using an overlapping step (*tap be po*) to face the center and do an double openline block (*sang kwi swa*). Do continuous stepping forward with the left leg and perform a double uppercut (*sang kiao*). Step back with the left leg and do a double hook (*sang kao*). Step back with the right leg and do a double pressing hand (*sang an chiu*). Evade to the left and execute an eyebrow height hand (*che bi chiu*). Evade to the right and execute an eyebrow height hand (*che bi chiu*). Step forward with the left leg and do a flick block (*tioh*) with the left hand, toward the center. Shift to the right leg and perform a rotating chop (*tsuan puah*) with the right hand. Close. Stand erect.

落地剪
DROPPING TO THE GROUND SCISSOR

踏左足左手開。踏右足進屈右手擋。呈身擒。換右足右手擋。疊退榻向右坐蓮。呈轉向前力士擋。閃左畔榻右手開弓。閃右畔榻左手開弓。翻向後右手開。踏左足左手開。並擒。踏右足雙掛入。疊退向中坐蓮。呈身雙擒。並扭。右足躂。左手切。右手釵。直進貫中拳。脫手雙豎拳。榻馬向前海底針。倒剪。反剪。盤左轉向前左抄右鞭。踏右足抱牌。扭進左足躂。並倒剪。反剪。進屈右足雙捘。呈身扭。進抱牌。退右足屈左手開弓。呈身擒。翻後屈右手開弓。呈身擒。平馬左手刈。跳進中指地。呈身雙挑。進左屈雙擒。進右屈雙擒。呈身退右足左手擒。右手切。翻前右擒。左手切。換左足左手挑。換右足右手轉破。收立正。

Step forward with the left leg and block down (*kai*) with the left hand. Step forward with the right leg into a kneeling stance (*kut be*) and do a right palm thrust (*t'ng*). Rise up and grab (*kim*) with the right hand. Shift to the right leg and do a right palm thrust (*t'ng*). Double step back into an overlapping stance (*tap be*) facing the right side. Sit in lotus posture (*che lien kut*). Rise while turning and executing a strong man thrust (*like shi t'ng*) to the front. Evade to the left by crossing the right leg over the left and execute a right open bow chop (*kwi kieng*). Evade to the right by crossing the left leg over the right and execute a left open bow chop (*kwi kieng*). Turn to face the rear and block down (*kai*) with the right hand. Step forward with the left leg and block down (*kai*) with the left hand. Immediately grab (*kim*) with the left hand. Step forward with the right leg and perform double hanging palms (*sang kwa lip*). Double step back to face the center, sit in lotus posture (*che lien kut*). Rise up and perform a double grab (*sang kim*) and immediately wrench (*liu*). Kick (*tat*) with the right leg. Slice chop (*chiat*) with the left hand. Side thrust (*tueh*) with the right hand. Follow with a straight forward center thrust (*kwan tiong*). Release and perform a double vertical punch (*sang kia kun*). Do an overlapping step (*tap be*) while turning and slide down facing the front in the needle beneath the sea posture (*hai twe cham*). Execute the falling scissor (*to chian*) and follow with reverse scissor (*wan chian*). Turn to face the front while the left hand grasps (*sha*) and the right hand does a backfist (*pian*). Step forward with the right leg while doing a holding the tablet strike (*po pai*). Wrench (*liu*) and step forward with a left kick (*tat*). Immediately peform falling scissor (*to chian*). And then do reverse scissor (*wan chian*). Rise to a crouching stance and perform double hold (*sang so*), then rise up and wrench (*liu*). Step straight forward with a holding the tablet strike (*po pai*). Step back with the right leg into a kneeling stance (*kut be*) and do left open bow chop (*kwi kieng*). Rise up and grab (*kim*) with the left hand. Turn to face the rear and then crouch while doing an right open bow chop (*kwi kieng*). Rise up and grab (*kim*) with the right hand. Switch to a bow stance (*kieng tzi be*) and smash (*kua chat*) with the left hand. Jump to a double kneeling posture (*chi teh kut*). Rise up and do double flicking block (*sang tioh*). Step forward with the left leg to a kneeling posture, performing double split (*sang li*). Step forward with the right leg to a kneeling posture, performing double split (*sang li*). Rise up, stepping back with the right leg while the left hand grabs (*kim*). Slice chop (*chiat*) with the right hand. Turn to the front, performing a right hand grab (*kim*). Slice chop (*chiat*) with the left hand. Shift to the left leg and flick block (*tioh*) with the left hand. Shift to the right leg and perform a rotating chop (*tsuan puah*) with the right hand. Close. Stand erect.

魁星手法
GOD OF SCHOLARS HAND

退楊右足魁星手。進左角挑。並開。踏右足右手貢。並掀。左手切。退右足左手擒。踏右足雙掛入。平馬右手盖。左手刈。左手盖。右手刈。踏右足抱牌。楊馬向後左手開。右手切。換右足右手開。左手切。楊馬向前雙批。換右足雙批。並扭。右足躂。左手切。右手釵。直進貫中拳。脫手雙豎拳。翻後左手擒。踏右足雙掛入。直進楊向前魁星手。進左足左手挑。換右足右手轉破。收立正。

Step back with the right leg to perform *Kwe Seng* hand. Advance forward to the left corner and flick block (*tioh*) with the left hand. Immediately block down (*kai*) with the left hand. Step forward with the right leg and hammer strike (*kong*) with the right hand. Then do a turning block (*hian*) with the right hand. Slice chop (*chiat*) with the left hand. Step back with the right leg and grab (*kim*) with the left hand. Step forward with the right leg while executing double hanging palms (*sang kwa lip*). Go into right bow stance and execute scooping block (*kay*) with the right hand. Left hand performs reaping elbow (*kua chat*). Left hand then does scooping block (kay). Right hand performs reaping elbow (*kua chat*). Step forward with the right foot and do holding the tablet (*po pai*) strike. Do an overlapping step with the right leg toward the rear and block down (*kai*) with the left hand. Slice chop (*chiat*) with the right hand. Shift to the right leg and block down (*kai*) with the right hand. Slice chop (*chiat*) with the left hand. Execute an overlapping step to the front with the right leg and execute a double slap hand (*sang pueh*). Shift to the right leg and do a double slap (*sang pueh*) and immediately wrench (*liu*). Kick (*tat*) with the right leg. Slice chop (*chiat*) with the left hand. Side thrust (*tueh*) with the right hand. Step straight forward with the right leg and execute right center thrust (*kwan tiong*). Release and then do double vertical punch (*sang kia kun*). Turn to the rear and grab (*kim*) with the left hand. Step forward with the right leg and execute double hanging palms (*sang kwa lip*). Step forward with the right leg and turn to the front such that the left leg is tucked in under the right leg in an overlapping stance. Execute *Kwe Seng* hand. Step forward with the left leg and flick block (*tioh*) with the left hand. Shift to the right leg and perform a rotating chop (*tsuan puah*) with the right hand. Close. Stand erect.

羅漢手法
LOHAN HAND METHOD

退寄左足羅漢手。進左手挑。並開。換右足右手挑。並開。換左足左手擒。踏右足右手破。疊退向右坐蓮。呈轉向前力士擋。進右足右手鞭。旋螺跳向前寄右足右手破。平馬左鈎右搖。踏左足抱牌。進左足蹴。平馬雙墜。吞手側插。坐節。左手開。右手開。換右足右手擒。左手切。退寄右手鈎。換左足雙鈎。扭進右足蹴。左手切。右手釵。向左畔左手掀。提右足掃向後平馬。右手開。左手開。踏左足左手擒。右手切。退寄左手鈎。換右足雙鈎。直進雙截。翻前左手擒。踏右足右手撟。退右足羅漢手。並左手挑。換右足右手轉破。收立正。

Step back into a left hanging leg stance (*kia ka be*) and execute lohan hand. Step forward with the left leg and flick block (*tioh*) with the left hand. Immediately block downward (*kai*) with the same hand. Shift to right leg and flick block (*tioh*) with the right hand. Immediately block downward (*kai*) with the same hand. Shift to the left leg and grab (*kim*) with the left hand. Step forward with the right leg and chop (*puah*) with the right hand. Double step backward and sit in lotus stance (*che lien kut*) facing the right side. Face the front and do a strong man thrust (*lek si t'ng*). Step forward with the right leg and backfist (*pian*) with the right hand. Execute a whirlwind jump to the front, hanging the right leg. Chop (*puah*) with the right hand. Step into right bow stance. Hook (*kao*) with the right hand and shake (*yao*) with the left. Step forward with the left leg while executing holding the table (*po pai*) strike. Step forward and kick with the left leg. Go into a horse stance and execute double falling punch (*sang tui*). Follow with swallowing hand (*tun chiu*), and side finger thrust (*chiak cha*). Sink the wrist (*che chat*). Block down (*kai*) with the left hand. Block down (*kai*) with the right hand. Shift to right leg and grab (*kim*) with the right hand. Slice chop (*chiat*) with the left hand. Step back with the right leg into a hanging stance and hook (*kao*) with the right hand. Shift to the left leg and double hook (*sang kao*), wrench (*liu*). Kick (*tat*) with the right leg. Slice chop (*chiat*) with the left hand. Side thrust (*tueh*) with the right hand. Face the left side and perform a left turning block (*hian*). Raise the right leg to sweep toward the rear into a left bow stance (*kieng tzi be*). Block down (*kai*) with the right hand. Block down (*kai*) with the left hand. Step forward with the left leg and grab (*kim*) with the left hand. Slice chop (*chiat*) with the right hand. Step back into a left hanging leg stance and hook (*kao*) with the left hand. Shift to the right leg and double hook (*sang kao*). Step straight forward and execute double intercept chop (*sang cha*). Turn to the front and grab (*kim*) with the left hand. Step forward with the right foot and uppercut (*kiao*) with the right hand. Step back with the right leg into a left hanging leg stance, executing lohan hand. Immediately flick block (*tioh*) with the left hand. Shift to the right leg and perform rotating chop (*tsuan puah*) with the right hand. Close. Stand erect.

Leonardo Co and Benito Tan

Volume 3
第三编

STANDARD PRACTICE METHODS
普通操練法

Tai Cho

Da Mo

Lohan

Pe Ho

Editor's Note: *The 38 forms described within this book are by no means the complete set of the existing Ngo Cho forms. Many well-known forms practiced by the different schools of Ngo Cho are not included, such as: Tit Kieng Chien ("Straight Arrow Battle"), Sang Sou Kun ("Double Roundhouse Punch"), Se Mun Kua Sau ("Four Direction Sweep"), Being Guat ("Moon Shine"), Pe Kuan Su Tong ("White Ape Exits from the Cave"), Tien Kong ("Monkey"), etc. These are all legitimate forms taught by the art's founder, Chua Giok Beng. Why these were not included in this book remains a mystery, for written documents of these forms might have been lost. However, movements from these forms are incorporated in the different techniques taken collectively in this book. Also, Ngo Cho's foundation form Sam Chien is incorrectly labeled in the book as Tit Be Chien ("Straight Horse Battle"). In reality, all Ngo Cho schools begin their training by doing the Sam Chien form. In this book, author Yu Chiok Sam instead places the form Ngo Ho Chien ("Five Tiger Battle") as the foundation form, and not Sam Chien. Personally, as a martial arts enthusiast, I believe that this book was intended to be used as a manual for regular, academic schools, and that Ngo Ho Chien was taught to address boredom in students, as it is more interesting than Sam Chien, which students may find less appealing.*

Following the teaching of my sifu, the late Grandmaster Tan Ka Hong of the Philippine-Chinese Beng Kiam Athletic Association, he listed 42 Ngo Cho forms and introduced two additiomnal forms. Within this book there are no forms attributed to the monkey style and only a couple attributed to crane, yet Beng Kiam has three monkey forms and five white crane forms. Perhaps these forms were not included in this book as they are more advanced or more strenuous. But, strangely and ironically, the secret technique considered one of the highest and deadliest secrets of Ngo Cho Kun, the Liok Mun Pat Wat ("Six Gates, Eight Methods") is included.

I enjoin my Ngo Cho brothers to assist in shedding light on the mystery of the missing forms in this "Bible." But I can attest to the authenticity of this manuscript, given knowledge of the Ngo Cho style of kung fu, which is the system I have embraced in my life as a martial artist.

五虎戰
NGO HO CHIEN

太祖派
TAI CHO FAMILY

FIVE TIGER BATTLE

踏足右手一拳。左手一拳。並扭。直進右手一拳。左手一拳。右手一拳。並
扭。直退左手一拳。右手一拳。並扭。向左畔退右足平馬左手擒。右手一拳。
踏右足右手擒。左手一拳。翻右畔右足踏角左手擒。右手一拳。踏右足右手
擒。左手一拳。向前方右足退平馬。左手挑。右手截。踏右足右手挑。左手
截。翻后方右足踏角左手開。右手切。踏右足右手開。左手切。翻前方右足踏
角左手鈎同時右手搖。踏右足雙批。並扭。右足躂。左手切。收抱牌立正。

Step forward with right leg, right *kun*, left *kun*, immediately *liu*. Step straight forward, right *kun*, left *kun*, right *kun*, immediately *liu*. Step straight back, left *kun*, right *kun*, immediately *liu*. Turn to the left side, pull back the right leg to a level horse, left hand *kim*, right *kun*. Step forward with right leg, right *kim*, left *kun*. Turn to the right side, right leg steps forward to corner, left *kim*, right *kun*. Step forward with right leg, right *kim*, left *kun*. Turn to front, pulling right leg backward to level horse, left *tioh*, right *chà*. Step forward with right leg, right *tioh*, left *chà*. Turn to the rear, step right leg forward to corner, left *kai*, right *chiat*. Step forward with right leg, right *kai*, left *chiat*. Turn to front, step right leg toward corner, simulatneous left *kao* and right *yao*. Step forward with right leg, *sang pueh*, immediately *liu*. Right leg *tat*, left *chiat*. Conclude with *po pai*. Stand erect.

This form is also called "Five Foundation Method" - Ngo Ki Lip Wat (即五技立法)

| 瑞華戰
SWI HUA CHIEN | |
| ELEGANT
BATTLE | 白鶴門
CRANE
FAMILY |

進右足雙陰插。並扭。雙鈎入。駿肚出。進左足雙陰插。並扭。雙鈎入。駿肚出。進右足雙陰插。並扭。雙鈎入。駿肚出。退右足左手擒。右手一拳。退左足左手擒。左手一拳。退右足左手擒。右手一拳。左手一拳。換右足右手一拳。換左足左手擒。盤手踏右足雙掛入。直進雙擋。並扭。退右足抱盤梭。退左足抱盤梭。直進右足抱牌。換左足抱牌。翻後方左足踏角右手開。左手切。換右足左手開。右切。踏右足雙手直進雙彈。並扭。翻前方右足踏角。左手鈎同時右手搖。踏右足雙捲。平馬右鈎左搖。踏左足雙批。換右足雙批。並扭。右足蹉。左手切。右手釵。閃右畔左手開。閃左畔右手開。退右足右手擋。踏右足和手挑。換左足左手挑。換右足右手轉破。收招揚手立正。

Step forward with right leg, *sang yim cha*. Immediately *liu*. *Sang kao lip*. *Chun to chut*. Step forward with left leg, *sang yim cha*. Immediately *liu*. *Sang kao lip*. *Chun to chut*. Step forward with right leg, *sang yim cha*. Immediately *liu*. *Sang kao lip*. *Chun to chut*. Step back with right leg, left *kim*. Right *kun*. Step back with left leg, right *kim*. Left *kun*. Step back with right leg, left *kim*. Right *kun*, left *kun*. Shift to right leg, right *kun*. Shift to left leg, left *kim*. *Pua chiu*, then step forward with right leg and execute *sang kwa lip*. Step straight forward, *sang t'ng*. Immediately *liu*. Step back with right leg, *po pua so*. Step back with left leg, *po pua so*. Step straight forward with right leg, *po pai*. Shift to left leg, *po pai*. Turn to the rear and step with left leg toward the corner, right hand *kai*. *Chiat* with the left hand. Shift to right leg, left hand *kai*. *Chiat* with the right hand. Step forward with right leg, *sang tua*. Immediately *liu*. Turn to the front and step with the right leg toward the corner, left hand *kao* and simultaneously, right hand *yao*. Step forward with right leg, *sang k'n*. Step into level horse stance, right *kao*, left *yao*. Step forward with left leg, *sang pueh*. Shift to right leg, *sang pueh*. Immediately *liu*. *Tat* with the right leg. *Chiat* with the left hand. Right hand *tueh*. Evade to the right side, left hand *kai*. Evade to the left side, right hand *kai*. Step back with right leg, right hand *t'ng*. Step forward with right leg, right hand *tioh*. Shift to left leg, left hand *tioh*. Shift to right leg, right hand *tsuan puah*. Conclude with *chiao yong chiu*. Stand erect.

鳳尾戰
HONG BE CHIEN

達尊派
DAMO
FAMILY

PHOENIX
TAIL
BATTLE

踏右足雙插。坐節。踏左足雙插。坐節。踏右足雙插。坐節。翻後方右足踏角左手挑。右手切。左手切。盤手踏右足雙掛入。翻前方右足踏角左手開。換右足右手開。退右足雙插。坐節。盤手踏右足雙掛入。退右足左手鈎同時右手搖。退左足右鈎左搖。向左方右足退平左手開。右手切。翻右方左足踏角右手開。左手切。向前方右足退平左手擒。踏右足雙倦手。直進雙弹。直退右手挑。左手挑。直進右手釵。收抱牌立正。

Step forward with right leg, *sang cha*. *Che chat*. Step forward with left leg, *sang cha*. *Che chat*. Step forward with right leg, *sang cha*. *Che chat*. Turn to the rear, right leg steps forward to the corner. Left hand *tioh*. *Chiat* with right hand. *Chiat* with left hand. *Pua chiu*, then step forward with right leg, *sang kwa lip*. Turn to front, right leg steps forward to the corner. Left hand *kai*. Shift to right leg, right hand *kai*. Step back with right leg, *sang cha*. *Che chat*. *Pua chiu*, then step forward with right leg, *sang kwa lip*. Step back with right leg, left hand *kao* and simultaneously right hand *yao*. Step back with left leg, right hand *kao*, left *yao*. Turn to left, right leg stepping back to an even stance. Left hand *kai*. *Chiat* with the right hand. Turn to right, left leg steps forward to the corner. Right hand *kai*. *Chiat* with the left hand. Turn to the front, right leg stepping back to an even stance. Left hand *kim*. Step forward with right leg, *sang k'n chiu*. Step straight forward, *sang tua*. Step straight forward, right hand *tioh*. Left hand *tioh*. Step straight forward, right hand *tueh*. Conclude with *po pai*. Stand erect.

| 六合拳
LUK HOP KUN | |
| SIX
HARMONY
FIST | 太祖派
TAI CHO
FAMILY |

閃左畔右手挑。左切。右切，閃右畔左手挑。右切，左切。平馬左鈎右搖。疊
進右足雙押，扭雙插。並扭雙鈎入。駿肚出。翻後方右足踏角左手開。踏右足
右手一拳。退右足左手一拳。換右足右手一拳。換左足左手擒。右手切。翻前
方左足踏角右手開。踏左足左手一拳。退左足右手一拳。換左足左手一拳，。
換右足右手擒。左手切，。右手切。平馬右鈎左搖。踏左足雙押中。扭雙插。並
扭。雙鈎入。駿解出。換右足右手挑。換左足左手挑。換右足右手轉破。收招
揚立正。

Evade to the left side, right hand *tioh*. *Chiat* with left hand, and then *chiat* with right hand. Evade to the right side, left hand *tioh*. *Chiat* with right hand, and then *chiat* with left hand. Step to an even stance, left *kao*, right *yao*. Double step forward with right leg, *sang kap*, immediately *liu*. *Sang cha*. Immediately *liu*, *sang kao lip*. *Chun to chut*. Turn to the rear, right leg stepping to the corner. Left hand *kai*. Step forward with right leg, *kun* with the right hand. Step back with right leg, *kun* with the left hand. Shift to right leg, *kun* with the right hand. Shift to left leg, left hand *kim*, and *chiat* with right hand. Turn to front, left leg stepping to the corner. Right hand *kai*. Step forward with left leg, *kun* with the left hand. Step back with left leg, *kun* with the right hand. Shift to left leg, *kun* with the left hand. Shift to right leg, right hand *kim*. *Chiat* with left hand, and *chiat* with right hand. Step to an even stance, right *kao*, left *yao*. Step forward with left leg, *sang kap* to the center. Immediately *liu*. *Sang cha*. Immediately *liu*, *sang kao lip*. *Chun to chut*. Shift to right leg, right hand *tioh*. Shift to left leg, left hand *tioh*. Shift to right leg, right hand *tsuan puah*. Conclude with *chiao yong chiu*. Stand erect.

茵藤踢
IN TIN TAT

達尊派
DAMO
FAMILY

ENTWINING
KICK

閃右畔左手開。右手切。閃左畔右手開。左手切。換左足左手擒中。踏右足茵藤梭。右足蹮。左手切。右手釵。直進貫中拳。退右足向右畔雙開綫。翻後方右手啄。並盖。左手鞭。換左足左手啄。並盖。右手鞭。退左足抱牌。提左足兩手夾胸並蹮。榻坐蓮向右。呈轉向後力士擋。踏右足右手貢。並掀。左手切。翻前方右足踏角左手擒。踏右足右手打節。並反墜。退右足左開右鞭。疊進左足左手挑。換右足右手轉破。收招揚立正。

Evade to the right side, left hand *kai*. Chiat with the right hand. Evade to the left side, right hand *kai*. *Chiat* with the left hand. Shift to left leg, left hand *kim* to the center. Step forward with right leg, *in tin so*. *Tat* with the right leg. *Chiat* with the left hand. Right hand *tueh*. Step straight forward, *kwan tiong*. Step back with right leg, turning to the right side, *sang kwi suan*. Turn to rear, right hand *tok*. Immediately *kay*. Left hand *pian*. Shift to the left leg, left hand *tok*. Immediately *kay*. Right hand *pian*. Step back with left leg, *po pai*. Lift left Leg, *sang kiap chiu*. Immediately *tat*. Overlapping *che lien kut* to the right side. Turn to the rear, *lek sit un*. Step forward with right leg, right hand *kong*. Immediately *hian*. *Chiat* with the left hand. Turn to the front, right leg stepping to the corner, left hand *kim*. Step forward with right leg, *pa chat* with the right hand. Immediately *wan twi chiu*. Step back with right leg, left hand *kai*, right *pian*. Double-step forward with the left leg, left hand *tioh*. Shift to right leg, right hand *tsuan puah*. Conclude with *chiao yong chiu*. Stand erect.

孩兒抱 HI LI PO	
CHILD HOLDING TABLET FIST	羅漢派 LOHAN FAMILY

踏右足抱牌。換左足抱牌。換右足抱牌。退寄雙鈎。直進雙撟。雙摽。駿肞。
疊進右足蹂。左手切。右手釵。換左足左手開右手搖。換右足右手開左手搖。
換左足左手開右手搖。退左足屈右手開弓。呈身右手擒。退右足閃左手開弓。
並左手擒。右手切。翻後方提左足榻進右足雙批。翻前方直進榻魁星手。進左
足左手挑。右手切。換右足右手挑。左手切。進左屈雙摛。進右屈雙摛。呈身
退右足左手擒。右手一拳。換右足右手擒。左手一拳。向左方右足退平左手
按。並盖。提左足駿蹂。翻右方左足踏角右手按。並盖。提右足駿蹂。向前
方。換左足左手挑。換右足右手轉破。收招揚立正。

Step forward with right leg, *po pai*. Shift to left leg, *po pai*. hift to right leg, *po pai*. Step back to a hanging leg stance, *sang kao*. Step straight forward, *sang kiao*. *Sang pioh*. *Chun to*. Double-step forward, *tat* with the right leg. *Chiat* with the left hand. *Tueh* with the right hand. Shift to left leg, left hand *kai*, right hand *yao*. Shift to right leg, right hand *kai*, left hand *yao*. Shift to left leg, left hand *kai*, right hand *yao*. Step back with left leg into a crouch, right hand *kwi kieng*. Rise up, right hand *kim*. Step back with right leg, evading. Left hand *kwi kieng*. Immediately left hand *kim*. *Chiat* with the right hand. Turn to the rear, lifting the left leg to overlap the right. *Sang pueh*. Turn to the front, stepping straight forward, *Kwi Seng chiu*. Step forward with left leg, left hand *tioh*. *Chiat* with the right hand. Shift to right leg, right hand *tioh*. *Chiat* with the left hand. Step left foot forward to crouch, *sang li*. Step right foot forward to crouch, *sang li*. Rise up, then step back with right leg, left hand *kim*. *Kun* with the right hand. Shift to right leg, right hand *kim*. *Kun* with the left hand. Turn to the left side, right leg stepping back to even stance. *An chiu* with the left hand. Immediately *kay*. Lift left leg, *chun tat*. Turn to the right side, left foot stepping to the corner. *An chiu* with the right hand. Immediately *kay*. Lift the right leg, *chun tat*. Turn to the front. Shift to left leg, left hand *tioh*. Conclude with *chiao yong chiu*. Stand erect.

Editor's Note: *Beng Kiam assigns this form to the "Monkey family"*

龍頭戰
LIENG TAO CHIEN

太祖派
TAI CHO FAMILY

DRAGON HEAD BATTLE

⊠⊠足雙陰插。並扭。雙墜。雙挑。坐節。退寄雙鈎。直進雙撟。雙摽。駿手。換左足左手啄。並盖。右手鞭。換右足右手啄。並盖。左手鞭。換左足左手啄。並盖。右手鞭。退左足雙批。換左足雙批。向右方左足退平右手擒。左手一拳。右手一拳。左手一拳。翻左方右足踏角左手擒。右手一拳。左手一拳。右手一拳。向前方左足退平右手擒。左手擒。右手一拳。收抱牌立正。

Step forward with ther right leg, *sang yim cha*. Immediately *liu*. *Sang tui*. *Sang tioh*. *Che chat*. Step back to hanging leg stance, *sang kao*. Step straight forward, *sang kiao*. *Sang pioh*. *Chun chiu*. Shift to left leg, left hand *tok*. Immediately *kay*. Right hand *pian*. Shift to right leg, right hand *tok*. Immediately *kay*. Left hand *pian*. Shift to left leg, left hand *tok*. Immediately *kay*. Right hand *pian*. Step back with left leg, *sang pueh*. Shift to left leg, *sang pue*h. Turn to the right side, left foot stepping back to an even stance, right hand *kim*. *Kun* with the left hand, *kun* with the right hand, and then *kun* with the left hand. Turn to the left side, right foot stepping to the corner, left hand *kim*. *Kun* with the right hand, *kun* with the left hand, and then *kun* with the right hand. Turn to the front, left foot stepping back to an even stance, right hand *kim*. Left hand *kim*, then *kun* with the right hand. Conclude with *po pai*. Stand erect.

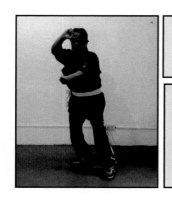

回馬搖 WAY MA YAO	
TURNING STANCE ROCKING PUNCH	羅漢派 LOHAN FAMILY

退寄左足羅漢手。直進左手挑。右手切。左手切。換右足右手一拳。退右足左
手搖。換右足右手挑。左手切。右手切。換左足左手一拳。退左足右手搖。退
右足抱盤挷。退左足抱盤挷。疊進屈右角雙摛。進屈左角雙摛。呈退左足右手
擒。左手切。換左足左手擒。右手切。踏右足右開左搖。翻後方右足踏角左手
鈎右手搖。踏右足抱牌。閃畔寄左足開弓。閃左畔榻右足開弓。在馬左轉向
後左手開弓。進右足躂。退右手切上。換右足雙批。翻前方提右足榻進左足雙
批。換右足雙批。並扭。右足躂。左手切。右手釵。榻跳轉向前雙搖。踏右足
抱牌。進右足屈左手開弓。呈身左手擒。退左足閃右手開弓。並右手擒。左手
切。換左足左手挑。換右足右手轉破。收招揚立正。

Step back to a left hanging leg stance, *lohan chiu*. Step straight forward, left hand *tioh*. *Chiat* with the right hand, then *chiat* with the left hand. Shift to right leg, *kun* with the right hand. Step back with right leg, left hand *yao*. Shift to right leg, right hand *tioh*. *Chiat* with the left hand, then *chiat* with the right hand. Shift to left leg, *kun* with the left hand. Step back with left leg, right hand *yao*. Step back with right leg, *po pua so*. Step back with left leg, *po pua so*. Double step forward into a crouch to the right corner, *sang li*. Step forward into a crouch to the left corner, *sang li*. Stand up, stepping back with the left leg, right hand *kim*. *Chiat* with the left hand. Shift to left leg, left hand *kim*. *Chiat* with the right hand. Step forward with right leg, right hand *kai*, left hand *yao*. Turn to the rear, right foot steps forward to the corner. Left hand *kao*, right hand *yao*. Step forward with right leg, *po pai*. Evade to the right side, into a left hanging leg stance, *kwi kieng*. Evade to the left side, into a right overlapping stance, *kwi kieng*. In the same stance, pivot to the left and perform a left *kwi kieng*. Step forward and *tat* with the right leg. Step back and *chiat* high with the right hand. Shift to right leg, *sang pueh*. Turn to the front, lifting the right leg to overlap the left. Step forward with the left leg, *sang pueh*. Shift to right leg, *sang pueh*. Immediately *liu*. *Tat* with the right leg. *Chiat* with the left hand, and *tueh* with the right hand. Perform a whirlwing jump to the front and perform *sang yao*. Step forward with right leg, *po pai*. Step straight forward into a crouch and *kwi kieng* with the left hand. Stand up, and *kim* with the left hand. Step back with left leg to evade. *Kwi kieng* with the right hand. Immediately right hand *kim*. *Chiat* with the left hand. Shift to the left leg, left hand *tioh*. Shift to the right Leg, right hand *tsuan puah*. Conclude with *chiao yong chiu*. Stand erect.

獅子翻身
SAI TZI WAN SIN

羅漢派
LOHAN FAMILY

LION TURNING BODY FIST

走馬向右角雙挼。向左角雙挼。退左足右開。左切。換左足左開。右切。向右
方左足退平右手啄。並盖。左手鞭。翻左方右足踏角左手啄。並盖。右手鞭。
向前方疊進右足抱牌。並扭右足蹺。疊退左足穿後方。並反剪。盤左轉向後抄
鞭。踏右足反搖。翻前踏右足撟。平馬左手開。右手開。踏右足雙押中。摔
斜。雙挑。坐節。扭雙擋。再扭。右手擋。左手擋。右手擋。翻後方左手擒。
換右足右手一拳。平馬左手窈肩。右手一拳。右手窈肩。左手一拳。踏左足左
手開。換右足右手一拳。翻前方右足踏角左手擒。右手一拳。退左足右手擒。
左手一拳。換左足左手挑。換右足右手轉破。收招揚立正。

Walking step to the right corner, *sang so*. Walking step to the left corner, *sang so*. Step back with left leg, right hand *kai*. *Chiat* with the left hand. Shift to left leg, left hand *kai*. *Chiat* with the right hand. Turn to the right side. Left foot steps back to form an even stance. Right hand *tok*. Immediately *kay*. Left hand *pian*. Turn to the left side, right foot steps to the corner. Left hand *tok*. Immediately *kay*. Right hand *pian*. Turn to the front and double step forward with the right leg. *Po pai*. Immediately *liu*. *Tat* with the right leg. Double-step back with left leg pierce to the rear. Immediately reverse scissor the legs. Coil left, rotate to the rear, *sha pian*. Step forward with right leg *wan be yao*. Turn to the front, stepping forward with the right leg, *kiao*. Step to an even stance, left hand *kai*, right hand *kai*. Step forward with right leg, *sang kap* to center. *Sut to*, *sang tioh*. *Che chat*. *Liu*. *Sang t'ng*. Again, *liu*. Right hand *t'ng*, left hand *t'ng*, and then right hand *t'ng*. Turn to the rear, left hand *kim*. Shift to right leg, *kun* with the right hand. Step to an even stance, left hand *tiao kian*. *Kun* with the right hand. Right hand *tiao kian*. *Kun* with the left hand. Step forward with left leg, left hand *kai*. Shift to right leg, *kun* with the right hand. Turn to the front, right leg stepping toward the corner. Left hand *kim*. *Kun* with the right hand. Step back with left leg, right hand *kim*. *Kun* with the left hand. Shift to left leg, left hand *tioh*. Shift to right leg, right hand *tsuan puah*. Conclude with *chiao yong chiu*. Stand erect.

雙龍抱印
SANG LIEN PO EN

DOUBLE DRAGON HOLDING THE SEAL

羅漢派
LOHAN FAMILY

踏右足右手啄。並盖。左手鞭。換左足左手啄。並盖。右手鞭。退左足抱盤搐右角。退右足抱盤搐左角。踏右足抱盤中。並雙墜。雙挑。坐節。換左足雙擋。換右足雙貢。閃右畔左手開。閃左畔右手開。換左足左手擒。踏右足雙掛入。疊退榻坐蓮向前。呈身雙擒並扭。右足躂。左手切。翻後方右足踏角左手擒。踏右足加刀剪。退寄雙鈎。扭進左足躂。並倒左側拔剪。反剪。鈎脚躂。進屈右足雙搐。呈身扭。進抱牌。翻前方提右足榻進左足反弓馬。並倒剪。呈左轉向前踏左角。左手抄右手鞭。踏右足反馬搖。翻後方提右足右手撟。翻前方直進右足屈左手開弓。呈身左手擒。踏右足右手刈節。並擋。換左足左手挑。換右足右手轉破。收招揚立正。

Step forward with the right leg, right hand *tok*. Immediately *kay*. Left hand *pian*. Shift to left leg, left hand *tok*. Immediately *kay*. Right hand *pian*. Step back with left leg, *po pua so* to the right corner. Step back with right leg, *po pua so* to the left corner. Step forward with the right leg, *po pua so* to the center. Immediately *sang twi. Sang tioh. Che chat*. Shift to the left leg, *sang t'ng*. Shift to the right leg, *sang kong*. Evade right side, left hand *kai*. Evade left side, right hand *kai*. Shift to left leg, left hand *kim*. Step forward with right leg, *sang kwa lip*. Double step back, overlapping the leg to sit in a lotus posture, facing front. Rise up, *sang kim*. Immediately *liu. Tat* with the right leg. *Chiat* with the left hand. Turn to the rear, right leg stepping to the corner. Left hand *kim*. Step forward with right leg, *ka to chian*. Retreat to hanging leg stance, *sang kao*. Immediately *liu*. Step forward and *tat* with the left leg. Immediately fall to the left side with leg scissors. Reverse the leg scissors. Hook the leg and *tat*. Step forward to a crouch with the right leg, *sang so*. Rise up and *liu*. Step straight forward, *po pai*. Turn to the front, lifting the right leg overlapping. Step forward with the left foot, *wan kieng chiu*. Immediately falling scissor. Rise up, turning to the front and stepping forward to the left corner. Left hand *sha*, right hand *pian*. Step forward with right leg, *wan be yao*. Turn to the rear, lifting the right leg, right hand *kiao*. Turn to the front, stepping straight forward with the right leg to a crouching stance. Left hand *kwi kieng*. Rise up, left hand *kim*. Step forward with right leg, right hand *kua chat*. Immediately *t'ng*. Shift to left leg, left hand *tioh*. Shift to right leg, right hand *tsuan puah*. Conclude with *chiao yong chiu*. Stand erect.

| 五技操手 NGO KI CAO CHIU | |
| 五祖拳 NGO CHO FAMILY | FIVE LIMB DRILLING HAND |

踏右足右手貢。平馬左手貢。右手撟。左手撟。換右足右手掀。並開。換左足左手掀。並開。換右足右手開。並擒。直進向後屈。呈身左手擒。換右足右手貢如前法。直進向前屈。呈身左手擒。換右足右手轉破。收招揚立正。

Step forward with the right leg, right hand *kong*. Step to an even stance, left hand *kong*. Right hand *kiao*, left hand *kiao*. Shift to right leg, right hand *hian*. Immediately *kai*. Shift to left leg, left hand *hian*. Immediately *kai*. Shift to right leg, *kai*. Immediately *kim*. Step straight forward, turn to the rear and crouch. Rise up and *kim* with the left hand. Shift to the right leg, right hand *kim*. Repeat the front method. Step straight forward, turn to the front and crouch. Rise up, and *kim* with the left hand. Shift to right leg, right hand *tsuan puah*. Conclude with *chiao yong chiu*. Stand erect.

Editor's Note: *This is the solo version of the "arm-banging" (kong ngo ki) drill.*

六門手法
LIUK MUN CHIU WAT

SIX GATE HANDS METHOD

五祖拳
NGO CHO FAMILY

插手。坐節。串拳。並罩。梱節。反摔。捲手。和鈎。按手。轉盖。摽節。並切。鈎入。駿出。

Cha chiu. Che chat. Ch'ng kun. Peng tao. Tee chat. Wan Sut. K'ng chiu. Ho kao. An chiu. Tsuan kay. Pioh chat. Peng chiat. Kao lip. Chun chut.

八法機 手 PAT WAT KI CHIU	
五祖拳 NGO CHO FAMILY	EIGHT METHODS HAND TECHNIQUE

第一法。雙掛手。進抱牌。直退右手擒。第二法。點左。點右。盤手搋。牛角
兜。第三法。開手搖。鳳眼手。貫中拳脫手雙豎拳。盤手迫肸。第四法。幫內
節。並抓塗駿肚出。第五法。摔肚進。左手脫。右手一拳。第六法。茵籐入。
貫中拳。盤手搋。第七法。掛枝入。對手斬。盤手搖。右手切。左手切。右手
割。抱盤。第八法。抱盤搋。鳳尾彩。並駿肚出。

(1) *Sang kwa lip.* Forward, *po pai.* Straight step back, right hand *kim.*
(2) Spot left. Spot right. *Pua chiu so. Gu kak tao.*
(3) *Kai chiu yao. Hong gan chiu. Kwan tiong kun, tung chiu, sang kia kun. Pua so, piak to.*
(4) *Pang lai chat.* Immediately *liao. Chun* to *chut.*
(5) Forward, *sut to. Tung chiu* with the left hand, *kun* with the right hand.
(6) *In tin lip, kwan tiong. Po pua so.*
(7) *Kwa ki lip. Dui chiu cham. Pua chiu yao. Chiat* with the right hand. *Chiat* with the left hand. Right hand *siat. Po pua so.*
(8) *Po pua so. Hong be tsai.* Immediately *chun* to *chut.*

直馬戰
TIT BE CHIEN

STRAIGHT HORSE BATTLE

太祖派
TAI CHO FAMILY

踏右足雙插。坐節。吞手。駿手。直馬三進三退如法。直進雙關。退寄雙鈎。
直進打節。並右手開。左手切。右手釵。收抱牌立正。

Step forward with the right leg. *Sang cha. Che chat. Tun chiu. Chun Chu.* Step straight forward three times and step back three times, repeating the same hand methods (sequence). Then step straight forward, *sang kwi chian.* Step back to hanging leg stance, *sang kao.* Step straight forward, *pa chat.* Immediately, right hand *kai. Chiat* with the left hand. *Tueh* with the right hand. Conclude with *po pai.* Stand erect.

Editor's Note: *This form is more commonly known as "Three Battles" (Sam Chien)* 三戰

天字戰
TIEN LI CHIEN

太祖派
TAI CHO FAMILY

HEAVEN CHARACTER BATTLE

踏右足雙陰插。扭雙墜。雙挑。坐節。吞手。駿手。直馬三進三退如法。直進雙關。退寄雙鈎。直進打節。並右手開。左手切。右手釵。收抱牌立正。

Step forward with right leg, *sang yim cha*. Immediately *liu. Sang tui kun. Sang tioh. Che chat. Tun chiu. Chun chiu.* Step straight forward three times and step back three times, repeating the same hand methods (sequence). Then step straight forward, *sang kwi chian.* Step back to hanging leg stance, *sang kao.* Step straight forward, *pa chat.* Immediately, right hand *kai. Chiat* with the left hand. *Tueh* with the right hand. Conclude with *po pai.* Stand erect.

Editor's Note: *This is more commonly known as "Heaven, Earth, Man Battle" (Tien Ti Lin Chien)*

| 左戰法
CHO CHIEN WAT | |
| LEFT
BATTLE
METHOD | 達尊派
DAMO
FAMILY |

踏右足雙插。坐節。踏馬三進三退如法。踏右足雙按。直進雙插。坐節。退右足左手鈎右手搖。退左足右手鈎左手搖。向左畔左手按。並盖。右手摽插。翻右畔右手按。並盖。左手摽插。向前左抄右鞭。踏右角右鈎左打。疊進右足雙按手。並雙插。坐節。吞手。駿手。退寄右手挑。左手挑。直進右手釵。收抱牌立正。

Step forward with right leg, *sang cha. Che chat.* Step straight forward three times and step back three times, repeating the same hand methods (sequence). Step forward with right leg, *sang an chiu.* Step straight forward, *sang cha. Che chat.* Step back with right leg, left hand *kao,* right hand *yao.* Step back with left leg, right hand *kao,* left hand *yao.* On the left side, *an chiu* with the left hand. Immediately *kay. Pioh chiu* with the right hand. On the right side, *an chiu* with the right hand. Immediately *kay. Pioh chiu* with the left hand. Turn to the front. Left hand *sha,* right hand *pian.* Step forward to the right corner, right hand *kao,* left hand *ta.* Double-step forward, *sang an chiu.* Immediately *sang cha. Che chat. Tun chiu. Chun chiu.* Step back to a hanging leg stance, right hand *tioh.* Left hand *tioh.* Step straight forward, *tueh.* Conclude with *po pai.* Stand erect.

Editor's Note: *This form is also called "Ancestor Battle"* 祖戰

鶴戰法 HO CHIEN WAT	
五祖拳 NGO CHO FAMILY	CRANE BATTLE METHOD

踏右足雙陰插。並扭。雙鈎入。駿肚出。踏馬三進三退如法。平馬向左角左鈎右打。踏右足右鈎左打。退寄右手挑。左手挑。直進右手釵。收抱牌立正。

Step forward with right leg, *sang yim cha*. Immediately *liu*. *Sang kao lip*. *Chun to chut*. Step straight forward three times and step back three times, repeating the same hand methods (sequence). Step into an even stance to the left corner. Left *kao*, right *ta*. Step forward with right leg, right *kao*, left *ta*. Step back to a hanging leg stance, right hand *tioh*. Left hand *tioh*. Step straight forward, *tueh*. Conclude with *po pai*. Stand erect.

挑截法
TIOH CHÀ WAT

FLICK AND INTERCEPT METHOD

羅漢派
LOHAN FAMILY

踏左足左手挑。右手截。踏右足右手挑。左手截。踏左足左手挑。右手截。翻後右手挑。左手截。踏左足左手挑。右手截。踏右足右手挑。左手截。翻前左擒。右手搖。踏右足右手擒。左手搖。踏左足左手擒。右手搖。退左足右手鈎。左手搖。退右足左手鈎。右手搖。向右畔右手開。左手切。翻左畔左手開。右手切。向前右手挑。換左足左手挑。換右足右手轉破。收招揚立正。

Step forward with left leg, left hand *tioh*. Right hand *chà*. Step forward with right leg, right hand *tioh*. Left hand *chà*. Step forward with left leg, left hand *tioh*. Right hand *chà*. Turn to the rear, right hand *tioh*, left hand *chà*. Step forward with left leg, left hand *tioh*. Right hand *chà*. Step forward with right leg, right hand *tioh*. Left hand *chà*. Turn to the front, left *kim*, right hand *yao*. Step forward with right leg, right hand *kim*, left hand *yao*. Step forward with left leg, left hand *kim*, right hand *yao*. Step back with left leg, right hand *kao*, left hand *yao*. Step back with right leg, left hand *kao*, right hand *yao*. Turn to the right side, right hand *kai*, left hand *chiat*. Turn to the left side, left hand *kai*, right hand *chiat*. Turn to the front, right hand *tioh*. Shift to the left leg, left hand *tioh*. Shift to the right leg, *tsuan puah*. Conclude with *chiao yong chiu*. Stand erect.

| 打角法 |
| PAH KAT WAT |

羅漢派	HITTING
LOHAN	THE CORNER
FAMILY	METHOD

踏右足右手插。坐節。退右足左手開。並擒。踏右足右手一拳。左手一拳。右手一拳。並扭。向左畔左手擒。踏右足右手撟。退右足屈左手開弓。呈身左手擒。踏右足右手貢。直進掀。左手切。向後左手擒。踏右足右手一拳。左手一拳。向右畔左手擒。踏右足右手撟。退右足屈左手開弓。呈身左手擒。踏右足右手貢。直進掀。左手切。向前平馬右手窋肩。左手窋肩。退右足雙插。坐節。盤手踏右足雙掛入。翻後左手擒。踏右足三拳。翻前左手擒。換右足右手一拳。收抱牌立正。

Step forward with right leg, right hand *cha. Che chat.* Step back with right leg, left hand *kai.* Immediately *kim.* Step forward with right leg, *kun* with the right hand, *kun* with the left hand, and *kun* with the right hand. Immediate *liu.* Turn to the left, left hand *kim.* Step forward with right leg, right hand *kiao.* Step back with right leg into a crouch, left hand *kwi kieng.* Rise up, left hand *kim.* Step forward with right leg, right hand *kong.* Step straight forward, *hian. Chiat* with the left hand. Turn to the rear, left hand *kim.* Step forward with right leg, *kun* with the right hand, and then *kun* with the left hand. Turn to the right side, left hand *kim.* Step forward with right leg, right hand *kiao.* Step back with right leg into a crouch, left hand *kwi kieng.* Rise up, left hand *kim.* Step forward with right leg, right hand *kong.* Step straight forward, *hian. Chiat* with the left hand. Turn to the front into an even stance, *tiao kian* with the right hand. *Tiao kian* with the left hand. Step back with right leg, *sang cha. Che chat. Pua chiu,* then step forward with the right leg and *sang kwa lip.* Turn to the rear, left hand *kim.* Step forward with right leg, and *kun* three times. Turn to the front, left hand *kim.* Shift to right leg, *kun* with the right hand. Conclude with *po pai.* Stand erect.

Editor's Note: *This form is also called "Hitting the Four Corners" (Se Mun Pah Kat)* 四門打角

二十拳
LI SIP KUN

TWENTY PUNCHES

太祖派
TAI CHO FAMILY

踏右足右手一拳。換左足左手一拳。換右足右手一拳。並扭。翻後左手掀三拳。翻前右手三拳。向左畔左手開三拳。翻右畔右手開三拳。向前左手擒三拳。踏右足右手擒二拳。收抱牌立正。

Step forward with right leg, right hand *kun*. Shift to the left leg, left hand *kun*. Shift to the right leg, right hand *kun*. Immediately *liu*. Turn to the rear, left hand *hian*, and right hand *kun*, left hand *kun*, right hand *kun*. Turn to the front, right hand *kun*, left hand *kun*, right hand *kun*. Turn to the left side, left hand *kai*. Right hand *kun*, left hand *kun*, right hand *kun*. Turn to the right side, right hand *kai*. Left hand *kun*, rigth hand *kun*, left hand *kun*. Turn to the front, left hand *kim*. Right hand *kun*, left hand *kun*, right hand *kun*. Step forward with the right leg, right hand *kim*. Left hand *kun*, right hand *kun*, left hand *kun*. Conclude with *po pai*. Stand erect.

| 雙綏法 |
| SONG SUI WAT |

羅漢派	DOUBLE
LOHAN	BANNER
FAMILY	METHOD

退右足抱盤梭。在馬雙拳。並左手擒。右手一拳。左手一拳。閃左畔右手開。
閃右畔左手開。閃角左手擒中。踏右足打節。並右手開。退右足左手擒。盤手
踏右足雙掛入。直退抱牌。榻馬向後左畔左手開。右手切。榻退向右畔右手
開。左手釵。右手一拳。左手切。向後左手擒。踏右足右手刈節。直進托上。
左手擋下。翻前左手擒。右手切。換右足右手擒。左手切。換左手擒。踏右
足刈節。直進右手托上。左手擋下。翻後左手擒。踏右足右手破。直進插。坐
節。退右足屈左手開弓。呈身左手擒。踏右足右手一拳。並扭。翻馬向前寄左
足開弓。踏左足扭。右足躂。退虎馬拳。踏右足和手挑。並屈右手開弓。呈身
右手擒。換左足左手挑。並屈左手開弓。呈身左手擒。踏右足右手撟。退右足
羅漢手。直進左手挑。換右足右手轉破。收招揚。

Step back with right leg, *po pua so*. In the same stance, *sang kun*. Immediately left hand *kim*. *Kun* with the right hand, and *kun* with the left hand. Evade to the left side, right hand *kai*. Evade to the right side, left hand *kai*. Evade to the corner, left hand *kim* to the center. Step forward with right leg, *pa chat*. Immediately right hand *kai*. Step back with right leg, left hand *kim*. *Pua chiu*, then sep forward with right leg, *sang kwa lip*. Step straight Back, *po pai*. Overlapping step to the left, facing the rear, left hand *kai*. *Chiat* with the right hand. Overlapping step to the right side, right hand *kai*. Left hand *tueh*. *Kun* with the right hand. *Chiat* with the left hand. Face the rear, left hand *kim*. Step forward with right leg, right hand *kua chat*. Straight forward, *tuh chiu* upwards. Left hand *t'ng* downwards. Turn to the front, left hand *kim*. *Chiat* with the right hand. Shift to right leg, right hand *kim*. *Chiat* with the left hand. Shift to left leg, left hand *kim*. Step forward with right leg, *kua chat*. Straight Forward, *tuh chiu* upwards. Left hand *t'ng* downwards. Turn to the rear, left hand *kim*. Step forward with right leg, right hand *puah*. Step straight forward, *cha. Che chat*. Step back with right leg into a crouch, left hand *kwi kieng*. Rise up, left hand *kim*. Step forward with right leg, *kun* with the right hand. Immediately *liu*. Turn to the front in a left hanging leg stance, *kwi kieng*. Step forward with left leg, *liu. Tat* with the right leg. Step back, *ho be kun*. Step forward with right leg, *ho chiu tioh*. Immediately crouch, right hand *kwi kieng*. Rise up, right hand *kim*. Shift to left leg, left hand *tioh*. Immediately crouch, left hand *kwi kieng*. Rise up, left hand *kim*. Step forward with right leg, right hand *kiao*. Step back with the right leg, *lohan chiu*. Step straight forward, left hand *tioh*. Shift to right leg, right hand *tsuan puah*. Conclude with *chiao yong chiu*.

三角搖
SA KAK YAO

THREE
CORNERS
ROCKING
PUNCH

達尊派
DAMO
FAMILY

退右足左手擒。右手切。左手切。盤手踏右足雙掛入。翻後左手擒。右手切。
換右足右手擒。左手切。退右足左手盖。右手切。左手切。盤手踏右足雙掛
入。直進右手切。左手切。翻前左手鉤右手斬。踏右足雙批。平馬右手鉤左手
搖。踏左足左手擒。右手切。左手切。平馬左手鉤右手搖。踏右足雙捲手。直
進雙彈。並扭。翻後左手鉤右手斬。踏右足雙批。平馬右手鉤左手搖。踏左足
左手擒。右手切。左手切。平馬左手鉤右手搖。踏右足雙捲手。直進雙彈。並
扭。翻前左手擒。右手搖中。疊進左足左手挑。換右足右手轉破。收招揚。

Step back with right leg, left hand *kim*. *Chiat* with the right hand. *Chiat* with the left hand. *Pua chiu*, then step forward with right leg, *sang kwa lip*. Turn to the rear, left hand *kim*. *Chiat* with the right hand. Shift to right leg, right hand *kim*. *Chiat* with the left hand. Step back with the right leg, left hand *kay*. *Chiat* with the right hand. *Chiat* with the left hand. *Pua chiu*, then step forward with right leg, *sang kwa lip*. Step straight forward, then *chiat* with the right hand and *chiat* with the left hand. Turn to the front, left hand *kay*, right hand *ta*. Step forward with right leg, *sang pueh*. Step to an even stance, right hand *kao*, left hand *yao*. Step forward with left leg, left hand *kim*. *Chiat* with the right hand. *Chiat* with the left hand. Step to an even stance, left hand *kao*, right hand *yao*. Step forward with right leg, *sang k'n*. Step straight forward, *sang tua*. Immediately *liu*. Turn to the rear, left hand *kao*, right hand *ta*. Step forward with the right leg, *sang pueh*. Step to an even stance, right hand *kao*, left hand *yao*. Step forward with left leg, left hand *kim*. *Chiat* with the right hand. *Chiat* with the left hand. Step to an even stance, left hand *kao*, right hand *yao*. Step forward with right leg, *sang k'n*. Step straight forward, *sang tua*. Immediately *liu*. Turn to the front, left hand *kim*. Right hand *yao* to the center. Double step forward, left hand *tioh*. Shift to right leg, right hand *tsuan puah*. Conclude with *chiao yong chiu*.

千字打
CHIAN LI TA

白鶴門
CRANE FAMILY

CHOPPING ATTACK

平馬向左畔左鉤右打。向右畔右鉤左打。榻翻向左角雙押。扭進雙插。再扭。雙鉤入。駿肚出。榻翻向右角雙押。扭進雙插。再扭。雙鉤入。駿肚出。退右足左手擒。踏右足雙破。直進雙彈。並扭。右足蹤。左手切。直進打節。並反墜。退右足左手托。並擒。踏右足雙扯剪。直進右挑。左手切。翻後左鉤右打。踏右角右鉤左打。榻翻向左角雙押。扭進雙插。再扭。雙鉤入。駿肚出。榻翻向右角雙押。扭進雙插。再扭。雙鉤入。駿肚出。退右足左手擒。踏右足雙破。直進雙彈。並扭。右足蹤。左手切。直進打節。並反墜。退右足左手托。並擒。踏右足雙扯剪。直進手挑。左手切。翻前左手擒。踏右足加刀剪。退寄雙鉤。並扭。左手切。右手釵。收抱牌立正。

Assume an even stance facing the left side, left hand *kao*, right hand *ta*. Face the right site, right hand *kao*, left hand *ta*. Overlapping step to the left corner, *sang kap*. Immediately *liu*. *Sang cha*. *Liu* again. *Sang kao lip*. *Chun to chut*. Overlapping step to the right corner, *sang kap*. Immediately *liu*. *Sang cha*. *Liu* again. *Sang kao lip*. *Chun to chut*. Right leg steps back, left hand *kim*. Step forward with right foot, *sang puah*. Straight forward, *sang tua*. Immediately *liu*. *Tat* with the right leg, and *chiat* with the left hand. Step straight forward and *pa chat*. Immediately *wan tui*. Step back with the right leg and *tueh* with the left hand. Immediately *kim*. Step forward with the right leg and *sang chi chian*. Step straight forward and *tioh* with the right hand. *Chiat* with the left hand. (Turn to the back and repeat the sequence). Turn to the front, left hand *kim*. Step forward with right foot, *ka to chian*. Step back into a hanging leg stance, *sang kao*. Immediately *liu*. *Chiat* with the left hand, and *tueh* with the right hand. Conclude with *po pai*. Stand erect.

This form is also called "Crane Method" (Ho Wat) 即鶴法

Editor's Note: *The literal translation of Chian Li Ta is "Thousand Character Hit." But because of the downward slope in the character, it refers to "chop," and thus is commonly called, "Chopping Attack."*

十字戰 SIP LI CHIEN	
CROSS PATTERN BATTLE	太祖派 TAI CHO FAMILY

踏右足右手一拳。左手一拳。並扭。直進右手一拳。左手一拳。右手一拳。直
退雙破。進打節。進抱牌。翻後左手擒。右手一拳。踏右足左手一拳。並扭。
直進右手一拳。左手一拳。右手一拳。直退雙破。進打節。進抱牌。翻前左手
擒。右手一拳。踏右足右手擒。左手一拳。踏左足左手擒。右手一拳。退左足
左手一拳。退右足右手一拳。退向左畔雙墜。向前寄右足雙串拳。平馬右手
盖。並一拳。退向右畔雙墜。向前寄左足雙串拳。平馬左手盖。並一拳。踏右
足抱盤梭。並雙彈。退寄右手挑。左手挑。直進右手釸。收抱牌立正。

Step forward with right leg, *kun* with the right hand, and *kun* with the left hand. Immediately *liu*. Step straight forward, *kun* with the right hand, *kun* with the left hand, and *kun* with the right hand. Step straight back, *sang puah*. Step forward, *pa chat*. Step forward, *po pai*. Turn to the rear, left hand *kim*, *kun* with the right hand. Step forward with right leg, *kun* with the left hand. Immediately *liu*. Step straight forward. *Kun* with the right hand, *kun* with the left hand, and *kun* with the right hand. Step straight back, *sang puah*. Step forward, *pa chat*. Step forward, *po pai*. Turn to the front, left hand *kim*. *Kun* with the right hand. Step forward with right leg, right hand *kim*, and *kun* with the left hand. Step forward with left leg, left hand *kim*, and *kun* with the right hand. Step back with left leg, *kun* with the left hand. Step back with right leg, *kun* with the right hand. Step back to face the left side, *sang tui*. Face the front in a left hanging leg stance, *sang ch'ng kun*. Step to an even stance, right hand *kay*. Immediately *kun*. Step back to face the right side, *sang tui*. Face the front in a right hanging leg stance, *sang ch'ng kun*. Step to an even stance, left hand *kay*. Immediately *kun*. Step forward with right leg, *po pua so*. Immediately *sang tua*. Step back into a hanging leg stance, right hang *tioh*. Left hand *tioh*. Step straight forward, right hand *tueh*. Conclude with *po pai*. Stand erect.

Editor's Note: *Also called "Three Battles Cross Pattern" (Sam Chien Sip Li)* 三戰十字

中縮法
TIONG KWAN WAT

太祖派
**TAI CHO
FAMILY**

**CONTROL
THE CENTER
METHOD**

退寄左足左手開弓。換右足右手貢。並掀。轉蓋。換左足左手貢。並掀。轉
蓋。右手摽插。踏右足左手摽插。退左足抱盤右角。退右足抱盤左角。退左足
抱盤中。換左足雙批。換右足雙批。換左足雙批。翻後右手啄。並蓋。左手
鞭。換左足左手啄。並盖。右手鞭。換右足右手啄。並蓋。左手鞭。退右足左
手擒。右手刈節。並啄。退左足右手擒。左手刈節。並啄。盤手疊進右足雙掛
入。翻前左手擒。進右足蹉。退右手一拳。進右足和手挑。換左足左手挑。換
右足右手轉破。招揚。

Step back into a left hanging leg stance, left hand *kwi kieng*. Shift to right leg, right hand *kong*. Immediately *hian*. Rotate to *kay*. Shift to left leg, left hand *kong*. Immediately *hian*. Rotate to *kay*. Right hand *pio cha*. Step forward with right leg, left hand *pio cha*. Step back with left leg, *po pua so* to the right corner. Step back with right leg, *po pua so* to the left corner. Step back with left leg, *po pua so* to the center. Shift to left leg, *sang pueh*. Shift to right leg, *sang pueh*. Shift to left leg, *sang pueh*. Turn to the rear, right hand *tok*. Immediately *kay*. Left hand *pian*. Shift to left leg, left hand *tok*. Immediately *kay*. Right hand *pian*. Shift to the right leg, right hand *tok*. Immediately *kay*. Left hand *pian*. Step back with the right leg, left hand *kim*. Right hand *kua chat*. Immediately *tok*. Shift to left leg, right hand *kim*. Left hand *kua chat*. Immediately *tok*. *Pua chiu*, then double-step forward, *sang kwa lip*. Turn to the front, left hand *kim*. Step forward and *tat* with the right leg. Step back and *kun* with the right hand. Step forward with the right leg, *ho chiu tioh*. Shift to left leg, left hand *tioh*. Shift to right leg, right hand *tsuan puah*. Conclude with *chiao yong chiu*.

朕頭法
TIM TAO WAT

SINKING HEAD METHOD

太祖派
TAI CHO FAMILY

走馬向右角鳳尾彩。摔尐。雙挑。坐節。雙擋。並扭。右手擋。左手擋。右手擋。退右足左手擒。右手一拳。退左足右手擒。左手一拳。退右足左手擒。右手一拳。並扭。走馬向左角鳳尾彩。摔尐。雙挑。坐節。雙擋。並扭。右手擋。左手擋。右手擋。並扭。退左足雙批。退右足雙批。直進右角右手啄。並蓋。左手鞭。換左足左手啄。並蓋。右手鞭。換右足右手啄。並蓋。手鞭。平馬左手擒。右手刈節。並脫手。踏右足雙押中。摔尐。雙挑。坐節。雙擋。並扭。右手擋。左手擋。右手擋。退右足抱盤拨。在馬雙拳。平馬左手蓋。右手刈節。右手蓋。左手刈節。踏左足雙鈎。換右足雙貢。直進雙啄。再進右手摔。翻後左手擒。踏右足右手開。退右足右擋。踏右足右手貢。閃右角右手擒。左手搖。換左足左手擒。右手搖。踏右足雙拨。進抱牌。翻前左手擒。踏右足葫蘆手。並閃右手開。直進和手掀。換左足左手挑。換右足右手轉破。收招揚正。

Walking step to the right corner, *hong be tsai. Sut to. Sang tioh. Che chat. Sang t'ng.* Immediately *liu. T'ng* with the right hand, *t'ng* with the left hand, and *t'ng* with the right hand. Step back with the right leg, left hand *kim. Kun* with the right hand. Step back with the left leg, right hand *kim. Kun* with the left hand. Step back with the right leg, left hand *kim. Kun* with the right hand. Walking step to the left corner, *hong be tsai. Sut to. Sang tioh. Che chat. Sang t'ng.* Immediately *liu. T'ng* with the right hand, *t'ng* with the left hand, and *t'ng* with the right hand. Step back with left leg, *sang pueh.* Step back with right leg, *sang pueh.* Step straight forward to the right corner, right hand *tok.* Immediately *kay,* and left hand *pian.* Shift to the left leg, left hand *tok.* Immediately *kay,* and right hand *pian.* Shift to the right leg, right hand *tok.* Immediately *kay,* and left hand *pian.* Step to an even stance, left hand *kim.* Right hand *kua chat.* Immediately *tung chiu.* Step forward with the right leg, *sang kap* to the center. *Sut to. Sang tioh. Che chat. Sang t'ng.* Immediately *liu. T'ng* with the right hand, *t'ng* with the left hand, and *t'ng* with the right hand. Step back with right leg, *po pua so.* In the same stance, *sang kun.* Step to an even stance, left hand *kay,* right hand *kua chat.* Right hand *kay,* left hand *kua chat.* Step forward with left leg, *sang kao.* Shift to right leg, *sang kong.* Step straight forward, *sang tok.* Again, step straight forward, right hand *sut.* Turn to the rear, left hand *kim.* Step forward with right leg, right hand *kai.* Step back with right leg, right hand *t'ng.* Step forward with right leg, right hand *kong.* Evade to the right corner, right hand *kim,* left hand *yao.* Shift to the left leg, left hand *kim,* right hand *yao.* Step forward with right leg, *sang so.* Step straight forward, *po pai.* Turn to the front, left hand *kim.* Step forward with right leg, *o-lo chiu.* Immediately evade, right hand *kai.* Step straight forward, *ho chiu hian.* Step straight forward, left hand *tioh.* Shift to right leg, right hand *tsuan puah.* Conclude with *chiao yong chiu.*

Editor's Note: *This form is also called "Three Times Hitting the Stomach" (Sam To Tim Tao)*

雙鞭法
SANG PIEN WAT

達尊派
DAMO
FAMILY

DOUBLE
WHIP
METHOD

閃右畔寄左足左手開弓。並扭。閃左畔換右足雙截。捲手。三拳。並扭。閃右畔換左足雙截。捲手。三拳。並扭。退寄左手盖。疊進左足反馬搖。並啄。轉盖。右手鞭。踏右足平馬左手開弓。並右手鞭。抱盤右。雙墜。踏左足擋。換左足左手開右搖。翻後右手啄。並盖。左手鞭。踏左足開弓。並左手啄。轉盖。右手鞭。踏右足平馬左手開弓。並右手鞭。抱盤右。雙墜。踏左足雙擋。閃榻向左雙摛。閃榻向右雙摛。換右足抱牌。翻前左手擒。踏右足右手沉。退寄和手擒。左手切。右手鳳眼。換左足左手挑。換右足右手轉破。收招揚。

Evade to the right side, into a left hanging leg stance, left *kwi kieng*. Immediately *liu*. Evade to the left side while shifting to the right leg, *sang chà*. *K'ng chiu*. *Kun* three times. Immediately *liu*. Evade to the right side while shifting to the left leg, *sang chà*. *K'ng chiu*. *Kun* three times. Immediately *liu*. Step back into a hanging leg stance, left hand *kay*. Double-step forward, *wan be yao*. Immediately *tok*. Rotate to *kay*. Right hand *pian*. Step forward with right leg to an even stance, left hand *kwi kieng*. Immediately right hand *pian*. *Po pua so* to the right. *Sang tui*. Step forward with the left foot, *t'ng*. Shift to left leg, left hand *kai*, right hand *yao*. Turn to the rear, right hand *tok*. Immediately *kay*. Left hand *pian*. Step forward with the left leg, *kwi kieng*. Immediately left hand *tok*. Rotate to *kay*. Right hand *pian*. Step forward with the right leg to an even stance, left hand *kwi kieng*. Immediately left hand *pian*. *Po pua so* to the right. *Sang tui*. Step forward with the left foot, *sang t'ng*. Evade with an overlapping step to the left, *sang li*. Evade with an overlapping step to the right, *sang li*. Shift to the right leg, *po pai*. Turn to the front, left hand *kim*. Step forward with the right leg, right hand *tim*. Step back to a hanging leg stance, *ho chiu kim*. Left hand *chiat*, right hand *hong gan chiu*. Shift to left leg, left hand *tioh*. Shift to right leg, right hand *tsuan puah*. Conclude with *chiao yong chiu*.

對粧法
TUI CHONG WAT

PURSUING FIST METHOD

達尊派 DAMO FAMILY

踏左足雙擋。並扭。換右足雙貢。換左足左手開。換右足右手一拳。並扭。翻後左手擒。踏右足右手上拳。換左足左手上拳。平馬右手下拳。左手下拳。右手中拳。閃左手窈肩。右手一拳。閃右手窈肩。左手一拳。閃左手窈肩。右手一拳。換左足左手開。踏右足右手一拳。翻前左手開。換右足右手開。退右足雙插。坐節。盤手。踏右足雙掛入。退右足左手開。右手一拳。退左足左手一拳。退右足右手一拳。踏右足抱牌。踏左足抱牌。踏右足抱牌。直進右拳。退右足左手挑。換右足右手轉破。收招揚立正。

Step forward with the left leg, *sang t'ng*. Immediately *liu*. Shift to right leg, *sang kong*. Shift to left leg, left hand *kai*. Shift to right leg, *kun* with the right hand. Immediately *liu*. Turn to the rear, left hand *kim*. Step forward with right leg, right hand *kun* (upward). Shift to left leg, left hand *kun* (upward). From a level stance, right hand *kun* (downward). Left hand *kun* (downward). Right hand *kun* (middle). Evade with *tiao kian*. Right hand *kun*. Evade with *tiao kian*. Left hand *kun*. Evade with *tiao kian*. Right hand *kun*. Shift to left leg, left hand *kai*. Step forward with right leg, *kun* with the right hand. Turn front, left hand *kai*. Shift to right leg, right hand *kai*. Step back with right leg, *sang cha*. *Che chat*. *Pua chiu*. Step forward with right leg, *sang kwa lip*. Step back with right leg, left hand *kai*. *Kun* with the right hand. Step back with left leg, *kun* with the left hand. Step back with right leg, *kun* with the right hand. Step forward with right leg, *po pai*. Step forward with left leg, *po pai*. Step forward with right leg, *po pai*. Step straight forward, *kun* with the right hand. Step back with right leg, left hand *tioh*. Shift to right leg, right hand *tsuan puah*. Conclude with *chiao yong chiu*.

連環法 LIEN KWAN WAT	
達尊派 DAMO FAMILY	LINKED RINGS METHOD

踏左足雙鈎。換右足雙撟。掇節。駿肐。換左足雙陰插。並扭。左足蹕。平馬雙墜。雙吞手。雙側插。雙坐節。再雙吞。雙側插。雙坐節。踏右足雙撟。雙盖。向右雙擸。踏左足左手擒。右手切。左手切。向左雙擸。踏右足右手擒。左手切。右手切。退右足抱盤挼。退左足抱盤挼。並雙彈。直進右足右手擒。左手擒。並打節。反墜。左手切。右手釵。並扭。右足蹕。左手切。直進右手一拳。並扭。翻後左手抄右手鞭。換右足右手擒。左手切。換左足左手擒。右手切。踏右足雙批。退右足右手擒。左手擒。進打節。反墜。左手切。右手釵。並扭。右足蹕。左手切。直進右手一拳。並扭。翻前左手擒。進右足蹕。退右手一拳。踏右足和手挑。換左足左手挑。換右足右手轉破。收招揚立正。

Step forward with left leg, *sang kao*. Shift to right leg, *sang kiao*. *Kwa chat*. *Chun to*. Shift to left leg, *sang yim cha*. Immediately *liu*. *Tat* with the left leg. Step to an even stance. *Sang tui*. *Sang tun chiu*. *Sang chiak cha*. *Sang che chat*. Again, perform s*ang tun chiu*. *Sang chiak cha*. *Sang che chat*. Step forward with right leg, *sang kiao*. *Sang kay*. Turn to the right, *sang li*. Step forward with left leg, left hand *kim*. *Chiat* with the right hand. *Chiat* with the left hand. Turn to the left, *sang li*. Step forward with right leg, right hand *kim*. *Chiat* with the left hand. *Chiat* with the right hand. Step back with right leg, *po pua so*. Step back with left leg, *po pua so*. Immediately *sang tua*. Step straight forward right leg, right hand *kim*. Left hand *kim*. Immediately *pa chat*. *Wan tui*. *Chiat* with the left hand. *Tueh* with the right hand. Immediately *liu*. *Tat* with the right leg. *Chiat* with the left hand. Step straight forward, *kun* with the right hand. Immediately *liu*. Turn to the rear, left hand *sha*, right hand *pian*. Shift to right leg, right hand *kim*. *Chiat* with the left hand. Shift to left leg, left hand *kim*. *Chiat* with the right hand. Step forward with right leg, *sang pueh*. Step back with right leg, right hand *kim*. Left hand *kim*. Step forward, *pa chat*. *Wan tui*. *Chiat* with the left hand. *Tueh* with the right hand. Immediately *liu*. *Tat* with the right leg. *Chiat* with the left hand. Step straight forward, *kun* with the right hand. Immediately *liu*. Turn to the front, left hand *kim*. Step straight forward and *tat* with the right leg. Step back and *kun* with the right hand. Step forward with right leg, *ho chiu tioh*. Shift to left leg, left hand *tioh*. Shift to right leg, right hand *tsuan puah*. Conclude with *chiao yong chiu*.

兩宜法
LIONG GI WAT

| TWO ELEMENTS METHOD | 羅漢派 LOHAN FAMILY |

閃右畔左手挑。右手切。左手切。閃左畔右手挑。左手切。右手切。換左手挑。並右手挑。閃屈左。呈身雙捲手。右足蹲。平馬左手擒。閃屈右。呈身左手擒。右手刈。踏右足雙鈎。疊進屈右角雙摘。進左屈雙摘。閃左手擒。閃右手擒。閃左手擒中。呈身退右手擋。並屈左手開弓。呈身左手擒。踏右足雙挨。並進貫中拳。脫手獨入拳。翻後左手擒。右手切。向右畔貫中拳。脫手獨入拳。向後左手挑。並屈開弓。呈身擒。換右足右手開。進貫中拳。脫手獨入拳。翻前左手擒。踏右足刈節。並右手擋。換左足左手挑。換右足右手轉破。收招揚立正。

Evade to the right side, left hand *tioh*. Right hand *chiat*, left hand *chiat*. Evade to the left side, right hand *tioh*. Left hand *chiat*, right hand *chiat*. Shift to the right leg, left hand *tioh*. Immediately right hand *tioh*. Evade to the left in a crouching stance. Rise up, *sang k'n chiu*. *Tat* with the right leg. Step to an even stance, left hand *kim*. Evade to the right in a crouching stance. Rise up, left hand *kim*. Right hand *kua chat*. Step forward with right leg, *sang kao*. Double step forward to the right corner into a crouch. *Sang li*. Forward to the left into a crouch, *sang li*. Evade, left hand *kim*. Evade, right hand *kim*. Evade, left hand *kim* (center). Rise up and step back, right hand *t'ng*. Immediately crouch, left hand *kwi kieng*. Rise up, left hand *kim*. Step forward with right leg, *sang so*. Immediately *kwan tiong kun*. *Tung chiu, tok lip kun*. Turn to the rear, left hand *kim*. *Chiat* with the right hand. Face the right side, *kwan tiong kun*. *Tung chiu, tok lip kun*. Turn to the rear, left hand *tioh*. Immediately crouch, *kwi kieng*. Rise up, *kim*. Shift to right leg, right hand *kai*. Step forward, *kwan tiong kun*. *Tung chiu, tok lip kun*. Turn to the front, left hand *kim*. Step forward with right leg, *kua chat*. Immediately right hand *t'ng*. Shift to left leg, left hand *tioh*. Shift to right leg, right hand *tsuan puah*. Conclude with *chiao yong chiu*.

Editor's Note: *This form is also called "Two Segments" (Liong Gi)* 即二節

地煞法
DI SAT WAT

五祖拳
NGO CHO FAMILY

COMET METHOD

閃右畔左手挑。右手切。左手切。閃左畔右手挑。左手切。右手切。換左足左手挑。平馬右手擒。閃屈
左。呈身雙捲手。右足蹤。平馬左手擒。閃屈右。呈身左手擒。右手刈。跳左足進中指地。呈身雙挑。向
左雙擒。向右屈雙擒。呈退右足左手擒。踏右足右手破。疊退向右坐蓮。呈向前雙捲手。右足蹤。左手
切。右手釵。進貫中拳。再進雙彈。退右足左手擒。踏右足刈節。榻馬開弓。在馬左轉向前開弓。進右足
蹤。退右手切。直進左手啄。並右手啄。退左足榻坐蓮向右。呈身向前雙搖。退寄雙鈎。扭進左足蹤。並
倒左側盤剪。反剪。鈎蹤。進屈右足擒。呈身扭。進抱牌。榻向後海底穿針。並倒剪。反剪。盤左轉向後
左手抄右手鞭。並左手擒。踏右足雙掛入。疊退向中坐蓮。呈身雙擒並扭。右足蹤。左手切。右手釵。榻
馬向左畔左手開。右手切。榻馬向右畔右手開。左手切。退右足左手擒。踏右足打節。反墜。退右足左手
開右手鞭。踏右足雙捲手。右足蹤。左手切。翻前左手擒。踏右足右手刈。並擋。換左足左手挑。換右足
右手轉破。收招揚立正。

Evade to the right side, left hand *tioh*. Right hand *chiat*, left hand *chiat*. Evade to the left side, right hand *tioh*. Left hand *chiat*, right hand *chiat*. Shift to left leg, left hand *tioh*. Step to an even stance, right hand *kim*. Evade to the left in a crouching stance. Rise up, *sang k'n. Tat* with the right leg. Step to an even stance, left hand *kim*. Evade to the right in a crouching stance. Rise up, left hand *kim*. Right hand *kua chat*. Step forward with left leg toward the center, pointing at the ground stance. Rise up, *sang tioh*. Face the left side, *sang li*. Turn to the right side in a crouching stance, *sang li*. Rise up and step back with the right leg, left hand *kim*. Step forward with the right leg, right hand *puah*. Double step back and face the right side in a sitting on lotus posture. Rise up, turning to the front, *sang k'n chiu*. Right leg *tat*, left hand *chiat*, and right hand *tueh*. Step straight forward, *kwan tiong kun*. Again, step forward, *sang tua*. Step back with the right leg, left hand *kim*. Right hand *kua chat*. Step overlapping, *kwi kieng*. Rotate left to face the front, *kwi kieng*. Step forward and *tat* with the right leg. Step back and *chiat* with the right hand. Step straight forward, left hand *tok*. Immediately right hand *tok*. Step back with left leg overlapping facing the right in a sitting on lotus posture. Rise up, facing the front, *sang yao*. Step back into a hanging leg stance, *sang kao*. Immediately *liu*. Step forward and *tat* with the left leg. Immediately fall to the left side into a side coiling scissor. Perform a reverse scissor, and then a hook kick. Move forward in a crouch with the right leg, *kim*. Rise up and *liu*. Step straight forward, *po pai*. Step overlapping to face the rear, then perform *hai tue chun cham*. Immediately falling scissor, then reverse scissor. Coil to the left to face the rear, left hand *sha*, right hand *pian*. Immediately left hand *kim*. Step forward with right leg, *sang kwa lip*. Double step back facing the center in a sitting on lotus posture. Rise up, *sang kim*. Immediately *liu. Tat* with the right leg. *Chiat* with the left hand. Right hand *tueh*. Step overlapping to face the left side, left hand *kai*. Right hand *chiat*. Step overlapping to face the right side, right hand *kai* Left hand *chiat*. Step back with right leg, left hand *kim*. Step forward with right leg, *pa chat. Wan tui*. Step back with right leg, left hand *kai*, right hand *pian*. Step forward with right leg, *sang k'n chiu*. Tat with the right leg. *Chiat* with the left hand. Turn to the front, left hand *kim*. Step forward with right leg, right hand *kua chat*. Immediately *t'ng*. Shift to left leg, left hand *tioh*. Shift to right leg, right hand *tsuan puah*. Conclude with *chiao yong chiu*.

四鳳法
SI HONG WAT

FOUR PHOENIX METHOD

五祖拳
NGO CHO FAMILY

踏右足封手入。進打節。反墜。榻馬開弓。翻左轉向前雙豎拳。翻向後雙豎拳。翻向前左手擒。踏右足右手開。退右足右手擋。並抱盤挍。疊進左足左手開。退左足左手擋。並抱盤挍。直進右足雙彈。扭進貫中拳。脱手雙豎拳。平馬挍右。提右足駿蹂。翻左畔左手盖。提左足駿蹂。翻向前雙批。疊進右足和手挑。疊退寄葫蘆手。並反馬搖。和手掀。進左足左手開右手鞭。換右足抱牌。換左足抱牌。換右足抱牌。退右足抱盤挍。退左足抱盤挍。退右足抱盤挍。疊進左足左手挑。換右足右手轉破。收招揚立正。

Step forward with right leg, *hong chiu lip*. Step forward, *pa chat. Wan tui*. Step overlapping, *kwi kieng*. Rotate to the left to face front, *sang kia kun*. Turn to the rear, *sang kia kun*. Turn to the front, left hand *kim*. Step forward with the right leg, right hand *kai*. Step back with the right leg, right hand *t'ng*. Immediately *po pua so*. Double step forward, left hand *kai*. Step back with the left leg, left hand *t'ng*. Immediately *po pua so*. Step straight forward with the right leg, *sang tua. Liu*. Step straight forward *kwan tiong kun. Tung chiu, sang kia kun*. Step to an even stance, so to the right. Lift right leg and *chun tat*. Face the left side, left hand *kay*. Lift left leg and *chun tat*. Turn to the front, *sang pueh*. Double step forward, *ho chiu tioh*. Double step back with *o-lo chiu*. Immediately *wan be yao. Ho chiu hian*. Step forward with the left leg, left hand *kai*, right hand *pian*. Shift to right leg, *po pai*. Shift to left leg, *po pai*. Shift to right leg, *po pai*. Step back with right leg, *po pua so*. Step back with left leg, *po pua so*. Step back with right leg, *po pua so*. Double step forward with the left leg, left hand *tioh*. Shift to right leg, right hand *tsuan puah*. Conclude with *chiao yong chiu*.

Editor's Note: *This form is also called "Four Segments" (Si Hong)* 即四節

雙爪法
SANG LIAO WAT

羅漢派
LOHAN FAMILY

DOUBLE CLAW METHOD

向左雙擒。向右雙擒。踏左足左手掀中。右手一拳。並扭。踏右足左手一拳。直進右手一拳。左手一拳。右手一拳。並扭。閃右畔左手挑。右手切。左手切。閃左畔右手挑。左手切。右手切。換左足手挑。換右足和手挑。直進封手入。進榻雙擒。翻後左手開。踏右足右手釳。翻前雙搖。退寄雙鈎。進右足躂。並雙彈。退右足向後右手開弓。在馬向前左手開弓。並擒。踏右足打節。反墜。退右足左手擋。並擒。踏右足雙扯剪。直進右手挑。左手切。翻後左手擒。踏右足雙扯剪。直進右手挑。左手切。翻前左手擒。踏右足雙貢。退寄雙鈎。右足躂。左手切。右手釳。換左足左手挑。換右足右手轉破。收招揚立正。

Facing the left, *sang li*. Face the right, *sang li*. Step forward with left leg, left hand *hian*. *Kun* with the right hand. Immediately *liu*. Step forward with right leg, *kun* with the left hand. Step straight forward, *kun* with the right hand. *Kun* with the left hand, and *kun* with the right hand, then immediately *liu*. Evade to the right side, left hand *tioh*. Right hand *chiat*, left hand *chiat*. Evade to the left side, right hand *tioh*. Left hand *chiat*, right hand *chiat*. Shift to left leg, left hand *tioh*. Shift to right leg, *ho chiu tioh*. Step straight forward, *hong chiu lip*. Step forward, overlapping, *sang li*. Turn to the rear, left hand *kai*. Step forward with the right leg, right hand *tueh*. Turn to the front, *sang yao*. Step back into a hanging leg stance, *sang kao*. Step forward and *tat* with the right leg. Immediately *sang tua*. Step back with the right leg to face the rear, right hand *kwi kieng*. Face the front, left hand *kwi kieng*. Immediately *kim*. Step forward with right leg, *pa chat*. *Wan tui*. Step back with right leg, left hand *t'ng*. Immediately *kim*. Step forward with right leg, *sang chi chian*. Step straight forward, right hand *tioh*. *Chiat* with the left hand. Turn to the rear, left hand *kim*. Step forward with right leg, *sang chi chian*. Step straight forward, right hand *tioh*. *Chiat* with the left hand. Turn to the front, left hand *kim*. Step forward with right leg, *sang kong*. Step back into a hanging leg stance, *sang kao*. *Tat* with the right leg. *Chiat* with the left hand. Right hand *tueh*. Shift to left leg, left hand *tioh*. Shift to right leg, right hand *tsuan puah*. Conclude with *chiao yong chiu*.

Editor's Note: *Beng Kiam assigns this form to the "Crane family"*

三才法
SAM CHAY WAT

THREE PARTS METHOD

五祖拳
NGO CHO FAMILY

踏左足雙擋。並扭。換右足雙貢。換左足左手開。換右足右手開。跳進屈右手擋。呈身擒。換左足左手開。換右足右手開。翻後左手擒。換右足右手開。進貫中拳。脫手獨入拳。退右足左手擒。踏右足右手刈。榻馬開弓。在馬左轉向後雙搖。換右足右手開。左手切。換左足左手開。右手切。踏右足雙捲手。直進雙彈。並扭。跳退抱牌。直進屈右手擋。翻前屈左手擋。呈身左手擒。進右足蹠。退右手一拳。踏右足和手挑。換左足左手挑。換右足右手轉破。收招揚立正。

Step forward with left leg, *sang t'ng*. Immediately *liu*. Shift to right leg, *sang kong*. Shift to left leg, left hand *kai*. Shift to right leg, right hand *kai*. Jump forward into a crouch, right hand *t'ng*. Rise up, *kim*. Shift to left leg, left hand *kai*. Shift to right leg, right hand *kai*. Turn to the rear, left hand *kim*. Shift to right leg, right hand *kai*. Step straight forward, *kwan tiong kun*. *Tung chiu, tok lip kun*. Step back with right leg, left hand *kim*. Step forward with right leg, right hand *kua chat*. Step overlapping, *kwi kieng*. Rotate left to face the rear, *sang yao*. Shift to right leg, right hand *kai*. *Chiat* with the left hand. Shift to left leg, left hand *kai*. *Chiat* with the right hand. Step forward with right leg, *sang k'n chiu*. Step straight forward, *sang tua*. Immediately *liu*. Jump back, *po pai*. Step straight forward into a crouch, right hand *t'ng*. Turn to the front, still in a crouch. Left hand *t'ng*. Rise up, left hand *kim*. Step forward, and *tat* with the right leg. Step back with, *kun* with the right hand. Step forward with right leg, *ho chiu tioh*. Shift to left leg, left hand *tioh*. Shift to right leg, right hand *tsuan puah*. Conclude with *chiao yong chiu*.

Editor's Note: *This firm is also called "Three Segments" (Sam Chay)* 即三節

鼓推鞭
KO TWI PI

羅漢派
LOHAN FAMILY

DRUMMER'S FLOG

退寄左足羅漢拳。進左手挑。並開。踏右足右手貢。並掀。左手切。退寄右手鈎。換左足左手開。並擒。右手切。退寄左手鈎。踏右角和手擒。扭進貫中拳。並雙豎拳。翻左畔左手掀。向後提右足掃平馬右手開。左手開。踏左足左手擒。右手切。退寄左手鈎。換右足雙鈎。盤手直進迫斛。 退右抱盤接。向右畔提右足蹥。平馬左手開。右手開。踏右足右手擒。左手切。退寄右手鈎。換左足雙鈎。盤手直進迫斛。 翻右畔抱盤接。提右足蹥。平馬左手開。右手開。踏右足右手擒。左手切。退寄右手鈎。換左足雙鈎。盤手直進迫斛。向後雙批。換左足雙批。換右足雙批。翻前直進榻魁星手。進左角挑。換右足右手轉破。收招揚立正。

Step back into a left hanging leg stance, *lohan chiu*. Step forward, left hand *tioh*. Immediately *kai*. Step forward with right leg, right hand *kong*. Immediately *hian. Chiat* with the left hand. Step back into a hanging leg stance, right hand *kao*. Shift to left leg, left hand *kai.* Immediately *kim. Chiat* with the right hand. Step back into a hanging leg stance, left hand *kao*. Step forward to the right corner, *ho chiu kim. liu*. Step forward, *kwan tiong kun*. Immediately *sang kia kun*. Turn to the left side, left hand *hian*. Sweep the right leg to the rear to end in an even stance, right hand *kai.* Left hand *kai*. Step forward with left leg, left hand *kim. Chiat* with the right hand. Step back into a hanging leg stance, left hand *kao*. Shift to right leg, *sang kao. Pua chiu*, then step straight forward, *piak to*. Step back with the right leg, *po pua so*. Face the right side and *tat* with the right leg. Assume an even stance, left hand *kai*, right hand *kai*. Step forward with right leg, right hand *kim. Chiat* with the left hand. Step back into a hanging leg stance, right hand *kao*. Shift to right leg, *sang kao. Pua chiu*, then step straight forward, *piak to*. Turn to the right side, *po pua so. Tat* with the right leg. Assume an even stance, left hand *kai*, right hand *kai*. Step forward with right leg, right hand *kim. Chiat* with the left hand. Step back into a hanging leg stance, right hand kao. Shift to left leg, *sang kao. Pua chiu*, then step straight forward, *piak to*. Turn to the rear, *sang pueh*. Shift to left leg, *sang pueh*. Shift to right leg, *sang pueh*. Turn to the front, step straight forward overlapping the leg for *kwe seng chiu*. Step forward to the left corner, *tioh*. Shift to right leg, right hand *tsuan puah*. Conclude with *chiao yong chiu.*

走底法
CHO TUE WAT

WALKING BOTTOM METHOD

羅漢派
LOHAN FAMILY

閃右畔左手挑。右手切。左手切。閃左畔右手挑。左手切。右手切。退右足抱
盤搋。疊進左手開。右手切。並屈左手開弓。呈身左手擒。踏右足雙捲手。進
抱牌。平馬右手盖。左手刈。左手盖。右手刈。踏右足抱牌。並扭右足蹠。左
手切。向左畔抱牌。並屈左手開弓。呈身左手擒。踏右足右手貢。並掀。左手
切。向後左手挑。換右足雙批。翻前屈左手開弓。呈身左手擒。盤手踏右足雙
掛入。翻榻向後左手開。右手切。翻榻向前右手開。左手切。翻後抱牌。並屈
左手開弓。呈身左手擒。踏右足右手鞭。退右足屈左手開弓。呈身左手擒。盤
手踏右足雙掛入。翻前魁星手。進左角左手挑。換右足右手轉破。收招揚立
正。

Evade to the right side, left hand *tioh*. Right hand *chiat*, left hand *chiat*. Evade to the left side, right hand *tioh*. Left hand *chiat*, right hand *chiat*. Step back with right leg, *po pua so*. Double step forward, left hand *kai*. *Chiat* with the right hand. Immediately crouch, left hand *kwi kieng*. Rise up, left hand *kim*. Step forward with right leg, *sang k'n chiu*. Step straight forward, *po pai*. Assume an even stance, right hand *kay*, left hand *kua chat*. Left hand *kay*, right hand *kua chat*. Step forward with right leg, *po pai*. Immediately *liu*. *Tat* with the right leg, left hand *chiat*. Face the left side, *po pai*. Immediately crouch and *kwi kieng* with the left hand. Rise up, left hand *kim*. Step forward with right leg, right hand *kong*. Immediately *hian*. *Chiat* with the left hand. Face the rear, left hand *tioh*. Shift to right leg, *sang pueh*. Turn to the front in a crouching stance. Left hand *kwi kieng*. Rise up, left hand *kim*. *Pua chiu*, then step straight forward, *sang kwa lip*. Step overlapping to face the rear, left hand *kai*. *Chiat* with the right hand. Step overlapping to face the front, right hand *kai*. *Chiat* with the left hand. Turn to the rear, *po pai*. Immediately crouch, left hand *kwi kieng*. Rise up, left hand *kim*. Step forward with right leg, right hand *pian*. Step back with right leg into a crouch, left hand *kwi kieng*. Rise up, left hand *kim*. *Pua chiu*, then step forward and *sang kwa lip*. Turn to the front, *kwi seng chiu*. Shift to left leg, left hand *tioh*. Shift to right leg, right hand *tsuan puah*. Conclude with *chiao yong chiu*.

清風法
CHIENG HONG WAT

羅漢派
LOHAN FAMILY

COOL BREEZE METHOD

翻右畔右手擒。翻左畔左手擒。翻前右手擒。換左足左手擒。右手一拳。並扭。踏右足左手一拳。並扭。直進右手一拳。左手一拳。右手一拳。退寄雙破。進榻雙擒。翻後左手開。踏右足右手釵。翻前雙搖。退寄雙鈎。扭右足蹉。並雙彈。退右足向後右手開弓。在馬向前左手開弓。並擒。踏右足打節。並抱牌。退右足左手鈎右手搖。退左足右手鈎左手搖。盤手疊進右足雙掛入。退右足抱牌挨。退左足抱牌挨。退右足抱牌挨。疊進左足雙批。換右足雙批。換左足左手鈎右手啄。退左足雙批。並扭。右足蹉。左手切。右手釵。閃右畔左手開。閃左畔右手開。退右足右手擋。踏左足和手挑。翻後左手抄右手鞭。換右足右手擒。左手切。換左足左手擒。右手切。踏右足右手開左手搖。翻前左手擒。右手搖中。疊進左足左手挑。換右足右手轉破。收招揚立正。

Turn right, right hand *kim*. Turn left, left hand *kim*. Turn to front, right hand *kim*. Shift to left leg, left *kim*. *Kun* with the right hand. Immediately *liu*. Step forward with right leg, *kun* with left hand. Immediately *liu*. Step straight forward, *kun* with right hand. *Kun* with left hand. *Kun* with right hand. Step back into hanging leg stance, *sang puah*. Step forward into overlapping stance, *sang li*. Face the rear, left hand *kai*. Step forward with right leg, right hand *tueh*. Turn to front, *sang yao*. Step back into hanging leg stance, *sang kao*. *Liu*. *Tat* with right leg. Immediately *sang tua*. Step back with right leg to the rear, right hand *kwi kieng*. *Kwi kieng* to front with the left hand. Immediately *kim*. Step forward with right leg, *pa chat*. Immediately *po pai*. Step back with right leg, left hand *kao*, right hand *yao*. Step back with left leg, right hand *kao*, left hand *yao*. *Pua chiu,* then double step forward and *sang kwa lip*. Step back with right leg, *po pai so*. Step back with left leg, *po pai so*. Step back with right leg, *po pai* so. Double step forward, *sang pueh*. Shift to right leg, *sang pueh*. Shift to left leg, left hand *kao*, right hand *tok*. Step back with left leg, *sang pueh*. Immediately *liu*. *Tat* with right leg. *Chiat* with left hand. Right hand *tueh*. Evade to the right, left hand *kai*. Evade to left side, right hand *kai*. Step back with right leg, right hand *t'ng*. Step forward with left leg, *ho chiu tioh*. Turn to rear, left hand *sha*, right hand *pian*. Shift to right leg, right hand *kim*. *Chiat* with left hand. Shift to left leg, left hand *kim*. *Chiat* with right hand. Step forward with right leg, right hand *kai*, left hand *yao*. Turn to front, left hand *kim*. Right hand *yao*. Shift to left leg, left hand *tioh*. Shift to right leg, right hand *tsuan puah*. Clonclude with *chiao yong chiu*.

Editor's Note: *Beng Kiam assigns this form to the "Crane family"*

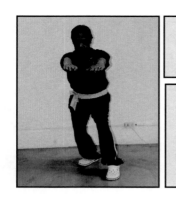

連城法
LIEN SHA WAT

LIEN SHA METHOD	達尊派 DAMO FAMILY

踏左足雙鈎。換右足雙鈎。雙摽。駿肸。換左足雙陰插。並扭。左足蹬。平馬雙墜。雙吞手。雙側插。雙坐節。再雙吞手。雙側插。雙坐節。踏右足雙撟。雙盖。鳳眼手。平馬左手盖。右手刈。右手盖。左手刈。跳左足進中屈指地。右手挑。左手挑。呈身右手擋。退寄左手按。並盖。退左足向左畔雙墜。雙吞手。雙側插。雙坐節。向前右手按。並盖。提進左足蹬。退榻坐蓮向右。呈轉向前力士擋。踏右足右手貢。並掀。左手切。向左畔左手按。並盖。右手摽插。向右畔右手按。並盖。左手摽插。向前左手抄右手鞭。疊進右足反馬搖。翻後踏右足右手撟。翻前左手按。並盖。向左角榻雙摛。向右角榻雙摛。換右足右手挑。換左足左手挑。換右足右手轉破。招揚立正。

Step forward with the left leg, *sang kao*. Shift to the right leg, *sang kao*. *Sang pioh*. *Chun to*. Shift to left leg, *sang yim cha*. Immediately *liu*. Left leg *tat*. Step to an even stance, *sang twi*. *Sang tun chiu*. *Sang chiak cha*. *Sang che chat*. Again, *sang tun chiu*. *Sang chiak cha*. *Sang che chat*. Step forward with right leg, *sang kiao*. *Sang kay*. *Hong gan chiu*. Assume an even stance, left hand *kay*, right hand *kua chat*. Right hand *kay*, left hand *kua chat*. Jump forward into a pointing at the Earth posture. Right hand *tioh*. Left hand *tioh*. Rise up, right hand *t'ng*. Step back into a hanging leg stance, left hand *an chiu*. Immediately *kay*. Step back with the left leg to face the left side, *sang tui*. *Sang tun chiu*. *Sang chiak cha*. *Sang che chat*. Face the front, and *an chiu* with the right hand. Immediately *kay*. Step forward and kick with the left leg. Step back and overlap the legs to sit in a lotus posture facing right. Rise up, rotating to the front, *lek sit tun*. Step forward with right leg, right hand *kong*. Immediately *hian*. *Chiat* with the left hand. Face the left side, left hand *an chiu*. Immediately *kay*. Right hand *pioh chiu*. Face the right side, right hand *an chiu*. Immediately *kay*. Left hand *pioh chiu*. Turn to the front, left hand *sha*, right hand *pian*. Double step forward to end with the right leg forward, *wan be yao*. Turn to the rear, stepping forward with the right leg, right hand *kiao*. Turn to the front, left hand *an chiu*. Turn Front, left hand *an chiu*. Immediately kay. Step overlapping to the left corner, *sang li*. Step overlapping to the right corner, *sang li*. Shift to right leg, right hand *tioh*. Shift to left leg, left hand *tioh*. Shift to right leg, right hand *tsuan puah*. Conclude with *chiao yong chiu*.

Volume 4
第四編

IMPROMPTU MOVEMENT METHODS
臨時運動法

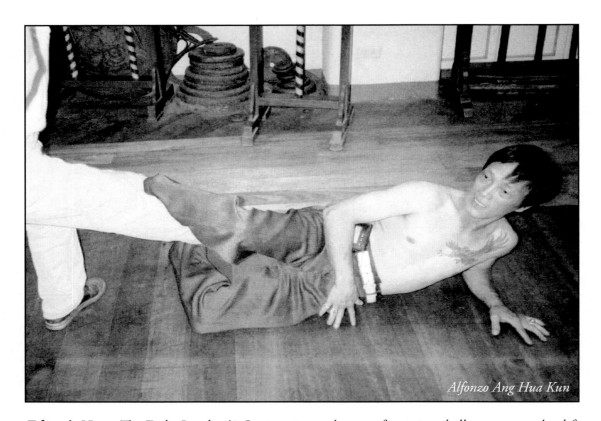

Alfonzo Ang Hua Kun

Editor's Note: *The Eight Levels, 48 Sections is another set of training drills extracting the different techniques of Ngo Cho Kun from the 38 forms that are presented wuithin this book. These Eight Level Drills contain 48 Sections of techniques that range from the basic to the advanced, such that these drills are more suited for advanced level students. A unique feature of this drill set is its focus on the gound fighting techniques of Ngo Cho Kun, which include techniques like the leg scissors and the knee-breaking squat (which is a very useful technique against the Northern long sweep).*

This set of drills also covers singular techniques emphasizing footwork and pivoting to the four directions. Further included is another version of the two-man iron forearm training drill called Kong Ngo Ki. Following Ngo Cho Kun traditions, the teaching of the empty-hand forms is to be limited and taught to suit the individual practitioner's physical build, features and characterisics. Essentially, the training drills presented in this section are like a shortcut to other forms; like a condensation of other forms' techniques to enable the students to have a preparatory, grasp of the Ngo Cho Kun system.

1 海底穿針法 – *Hai Tue Chung Cham Wat*
Sea Bottom Piercing Needle Method

疊進右足雙批。旋螺跳向前雙破。跳向後雙批。榻跳向前穿針。並倒剪。反剪。翻向前右手鞭。踏馬右足反馬搖。翻後踏右足橋。翻前屈左手開弓。呈身擒。踏右足破。收立正。

Starting with the right leg, double step forward. *Sang pueh*. Whirlwind jump to the front, *sang puah*. Jump to the rear, *sang pueh*. Overlapping step and then jump to the front, into the needle piercing-sea-bottom posture. Immediately side scissor, then reverse scissor. Turn to the front and *pian* with the right hand. Step forward with the right leg, *wan be yao*. Turn to the rear, stepping forward with the right leg, right hand *kiao*. Turn to the front in a crouching stance, left hand *kwi kieng*. Rise up and *kim*. Step forward with the right leg, *puah*. Conclude. Stand erect.

2 指地坐蓮法 – *Tze Teh Che Lien Wat*
Pointing at the Ground, Sitting Lotus Method

跳進左足平馬指地。呈身雙挑。進左屈雙擒。進右屈雙擒。呈身退右足左手擒。踏右足雙掛入。疊退向前坐蓮。呈身雙擒。並扭右足躂。左手切。右手釵。收立正。

Jump forward with the left leg into an even stance. Assume the pointing-at-the-ground posture. Rise up, *sang tioh*. Step forward with the left leg into a crouch, *sang li*. Step forward with the right leg into a crouch, *sang li*. Rise up, stepping back with the right leg, left hand *kim*. Step forward with the right leg, *sang kwa lip*. Double step back into a sitting-on-lotus posture facing the front. Rise up, *sang kim*. Immediately *liu*. Right leg *tat*, left hand *chiat*, right hand *tueh*. Conclude. Stand erect.

3 開切盤轉法 – *Kai Chat Puan Tsuan Wat*
Down Block and Chop, Coil and Rotate Method

踏左足左手開。右手切。退左足右手開。左手切。楊馬向後踏左足左手開。右手切。退左足右手開。左手切。楊馬向前踏左足左手開。右手切。退左足右手開。左手切。右手釽。收立正。

Step forward with the left leg, left hand *kai*, right hand *chiat*. Step back with the left leg, right hand *kai*, left hand *chiat*. Do overlapping step to face the rear and then step forward with the left leg. Left hand *kai*, right hand *chiat*. Step back with the left leg, right hand *kai*, left hand *chiat*. Overlapping step to face the front and then step forward with the left leg. Left hand *kai*, right hand *chiat*. Step back with the left leg, right hand *kai*, left hand *chiat*, right hand *tueh*. Conclude. Stand erect.

4 雙摔四門法 – *Sang Sut Se Mun Wat*
Double Stomach Slap, Four Doors Method

踏右足雙夾。並雙摔。退左足向左畔雙夾。並雙摔。退左足向後方雙夾。並雙摔。再退向右畔雙夾。並雙摔。退向前雙夾。並雙摔。收立正。

Step forward with the right leg, *sang kiap*. Immediately *sang sut*. Step back with the left leg to face the left side, *sang kiap*. Immediately *sang sut*. Step back with the left leg to face the rear, *sang kiap*. Immediately *sang sut*. Repeat again to the right side, *sang kiap*. Immediately *sang sut*. Retreat to face the front, *sang kiap*. Immediately *sang sut*. Conclude. Stand erect.

5 開弓榻馬法 – *Kwi Kieng Tap Be Wat*
Open Bow Chop, Overlapping Horse Method

疊進左手開弓。閃榻右手開弓。在馬左轉向前開弓。進右足躂。退右手切。並屈左手開。呈身擒。換右足轉破。收立正。

Double step forward, left hand *kwi kieng*. Evade with overlapping step, right hand *kwi kieng*. In the same stance, rotate left to face the front, *kwi kieng*. Step forward, right leg *tat*. Step back, right hand *chiat*. Immediately crouch, left hand *kai*. Rise up, *kim*. Shift to the right leg, *tsuan puah*. Conclude. Stand erect.

6 雙擒前後屈 – *Sang Kim Tsue Au Kut*
Double Grab, Front and Rear Crouch

踏左足擒。踏右足撟。退右足屈。呈身擒。換右足開。並擒。直進屈向後。呈身擒。踏右足撟。如前法翻前至開擒。收立正。

Step forward, left hand *kim*. Step forward, right hand *kiao*. Step back with the right leg into a crouch. Rise up, *kim*. Shift to the right leg, *kai*. Immediately *kim*. Step straight forward into a crouch facing the rear. Rise up, *kim*. Step forward, right hand *kiao*. Repeat the front method to the rear, until *kai kim*. Conclude. Stand erect.

1

擒手進退法 – *Kim Chiu Jin Teh Wat*
Grab Hand, Advance and Retreat Method

踏左足左手擒。退左足右手擒。進左足左手擒。踏右足右手擒。退右足左手擒。進右足右手擒。收立正。

Step forward with the left leg, left hand *kim*. Step back with the left leg, right hand *kim*. Forward with the left leg, left hand *kim*. Step forward with the right leg, right hand *kim*. Step back with the right leg, left hand *kim*. Forward with the right leg, right hand *kim*. Conclude. Stand erect.

2

掀手四門法 – *Hian Chiu Se Mun Wat*
Turning Hand, Four Doors Method

踏左足左手掀。踏右足右手掀。向左畔掀。踏右足掀。向後掀。踏右足掀。向右畔掀。踏右足掀。向前掀。踏右足掀。收立正。

Step forward with the left leg, left hand *hian*. Step forward with right leg, right hand *hian*. Face the left side, *hian*. Step forward, right hand *hian*. Face the rear, *hian*. Step forward, right hand *hian*. Face the right side, *hian*. Step forward, right hand *hian*. Face the front, *hian*. Step forward, right hand *hian*. Conclude. Stand erect.

3

開弓前後屈 – *Kwi Kieng Tsui Au Kut*
Open Bow Chop, Front and Rear Crouch

退右足屈左手開弓。呈身擒。退左足屈右手開弓。呈身擒。直進向後屈。呈身
左手擒。退右足屈。呈身右手擒。直進向前屈。呈身左手擒。換右足右手轉
破。收立正。

Step back with the right leg into a crouch, left hand *kwi kieng*. Rise up, *kim*. Step back with the left leg into a crouch, right hand *kwi kieng*. Rise up, *kim*. Step straight forward into a crouch, facing the rear. Rise up, left hand *kim*. Step back with the right leg into a crouch. Rise up, right hand *kim*. Step straight forward into a crouch, facing the front. Rise up, left hand *kim*. Shift to the right leg, right hand *tsuan puah*. Conclude. Stand erect.

4

按手雙轉法 – *An Chiu Sang Tsuan Wat*
Pressing Hand, Double Rotating Method

踏右足右手按。向左畔左手按。翻右畔右手按。向前左手按。踏右足右手按。
再轉如法。收立正。

Step forward with right leg, right hand *an chiu*. Face the left side, left hand *an chiu*. Face the rear, right hand *an chiu*. Face the front, left hand *an chiu*. Step forward with right leg, right hand *an chiu*. Repeat this method, rotating again. Conclude. Stand erect.

5

雙批旋螺跳 – *Sang Pue Sui Tsuan Tiao*
Double Slapping Hand, Whirlwind Jump

疊進右足雙批。旋螺跳向前雙破。跳向後雙批。旋螺跳向後雙破。跳向前雙批。收立正。

Starting with right leg, double step forward, *sang pueh*. Whirlwind jump, still facing the front, *sang puah*. Jump to face the rear, *sang pueh*. Whirlwind jump, still facing the rear, *sang puah*. Jump to face the front, *sang pueh*. Conclude. Stand erect.

6

抱牌前後跳 – *Po Pai Tsue Au Tiao*
Tablet Holding Strike, Front and Rear Jump

踏右足抱牌。跳向後抱牌。跳向前抱牌。向左畔抱牌。翻右畔抱牌。向前抱牌。換右足抱牌。收立正。

Step forward with right leg, *po pai*. Jump to face the rear, *po pai*. Jump to face the front, *po pai*. Face the left side, *po pai*. Face the right side, *po pai*. Face the front, *po pai*. Shift to the right leg, *po pai*. Conclude. Stand erect.

1

雙批十字榻 – *Sang Pueh Sip Li Tap*
Double Slapping Hand, Cross Pattern Overlapping Step

踏右足雙批。榻馬向後雙批。榻馬向前雙批。榻馬向左畔雙批。榻馬向右畔雙批。退右足向前雙批。踏右足雙批。收立正。

Step forward with right leg, *sang pueh*. Overlapping step to face rear, *sang pueh*. Overlapping step to face front, *sang pueh*. Overlapping step to face the left side, *sang pueh*. Overlapping step to face the right side, *sang pueh*. Overlapping step to face front, *sang pueh*. Step forward with right leg, *sang pueh*. Conclude. Stand erect.

2

開綫四門法 – *Kwi Suan Se Mun Wat*
Open Line Block, Four Doors Method

踏右足雙開綫。退右足向右畔雙開綫。退向後方雙開綫。退向左畔雙開綫。退向前雙開綫。進右足。並雙開綫。收立正。

Step forward with right leg, *sang kwi suan*. Step back with right leg to face the right side, *sang kwi suan*. Turn to face rear, *sang kwi suan*. Turn to face the left side, *sang kwi suan*. Turn to face front, *sang kwi suan*. Step forward with right leg, immediately *sang kwi suan*. Conclude. Stand erect.

3 開手四門法 – *Kai Chiu Se Mun Wat*
Down Block, Four Doors Method

踏右足開。踏左足開。向右畔開。踏左足開。向後方開。踏左足開。向左畔開。踏左足開。向前右手開。踏左足開。退左足右手一拳。收立正。

Step forward with right leg, *kai*. Step forward with left leg, *kai*. Face the right side, *kai*. Step forward with left leg, *kai*. Face the rear, *kai*. Step forward with left leg, *kai*. Face the left side, *kai*. Step forward with left leg, *kai*. Face the front, *kai*. Step forward with left leg, *kai*. Step back with the left leg, right hand *kun*. Conclude. Stand erect.

4 挑屈前後法 – *Tioh Kut Tsui Au Wat*
Kneeling Flick Block, Front and Rear Method

踏左足左手挑。並屈。呈身擒。換右足右手開。並擒。直進屈向後左手開。呈身擒。換右足右手挑。並屈。呈身擒。直進屈向前左手開。呈身擒。換右足右手轉破。收立正。

Step forward with left leg, left hand *tioh*. Immediately crouch. Rise up, *kim*. Shift to right leg, right hand *kai*. Immediately *kim*. Step straight forward into a crouch facing the rear, left hand *kai*. Rise up, *kim*. Shift to right leg, right hand *tioh*. Immediately crouch. Rise up, *kim*. Step straight forward into a crouch facing the front, left hand *kai*. Rise up, *kim*. Shift to right leg, right hand *tsuan puah*. Conclude. Stand erect.

第三段
THIRD LEVEL

5

角節坐蓮法 – *Kak Chat Che Lien Wat*
Corner Elbow, Sitting Lotus Method

踏左足平馬雙角節。並雙摔。疊進向前坐蓮。呈身雙扭右足躂。左手切。右手銳。翻後左手擒。踏右足雙掛入。疊退向中坐蓮。呈身雙扭躂。左手切。右手銳。翻前擒。換右足破。收立正。

Step forward with left leg into an even stance, sang *kak chat*. Immediately *sang sut*. Double step forward into a sitting on lotus posture facing the front. Rise up, *sang liu*. Right leg *tat*, left hand *chiat*, right hand *tueh*. Turn to the rear, left hand *kim*. Step forward with right leg, *sang kwa lip*. Take a double step back to face the center in a sitting on- otus posture. Rise up, *sang liu*, and *tat*. Left hand *chiat*, right hand *tueh*. Turn to the front, *kim*. Shift to right leg, *tsuan puah*. Conclude. Stand erect.

6

雙離力士法 – *Sang Li Liak Si Wat*
Double Split Strong Man Method

進左屈雙攜。進右屈雙攜。再進左進右如法。呈身退右足左手擒。踏右足右手破。退榻向右坐蓮。轉屈左手擋。呈身擒。踏右足屈右手擋。呈身擒。換左足挑。換右足轉破。收立正。

Step forward with left leg into a crouch, *sang li*. Step forward with right leg into a crouch, *sang li*. Repeat moving forward to the left and right, repeating the same methods. Rise up, stepping back with right leg, left hand *kim*. Step forward with right leg, right hand *puah*. Step back, overlapping into a sitting on lotus posture, facing the right side. Rotate into a crouch, left hand *t'ng*. Rise up, *kim*. Shift to the left leg, *tioh*. Shift to the right leg, *tsuan puah*. Conclude. Stand erect.

1 雙批盤轉法 – *Sang Pueh Puan Tsuan Wat*
Double Slap Hand, Coil and Rotate Method

疊進右足雙批。退右足雙批。榻馬向後雙批。退右足雙批。榻馬向前雙批。榻馬向左畔雙批。榻馬向右畔雙批。退右足雙批中。收立正。

Starting with the right leg, double step forward, *sang pueh*. Step back with right leg, *sang pueh*. Overlapping step to face the rear, *sang pueh*. Step back with right leg, *sang pueh*. Overlapping step to face the front, *sang pueh*. Overlapping step to face the left side, *sang pueh*. Overlapping step to face the right side, *sang pueh*. Step back with right leg, *sang pueh* to the center. Conclude. Stand erect.

2 開手榻轉法 – *Kai Chiu Tap Tsuan Wat*
Down Block, Overlapping Rotate Method

榻右足開。榻左足開。向右畔。向後方。向左畔。向前方如法。換右足右手一拳。收立正。

Overlap right leg, *kai*. Overlap left leg, *kai*. Repeat the same method to the right side, then the rear, the left side and the front. Step back with the right leg, right hand *kun*. Conclude. Stand erect.

3

雙離榻馬法 – *Sang Li Tap Be Wat*
Double Splitting Block, Overlapping Step Method

向左榻雙摛。向右榻雙摛。閃向左雙摛。閃向右雙摛。踏左足左手擒。踏右足右手撟。退馬屈。呈身擒。換右足轉破。收立正。

Do an overlapping step to face left, *sang li*. Overlapping step to face the right, *sang li*. Evade and face the left, *sang li*. Evade and face the right, *sang li*. Step forward with left leg, left hand *kim*. Step forward with right leg, right hand *kiao*. Step back into a crouch. Rise up, *kim*. Shift to right leg, *tsuan puah*. Conclude. Stand erect.

4

力士坐蓮法 – *Lek Si Che Lian Wat*
Strong Man Hold, Sitting Lotus Method

踏右足右手鞭。退榻向右坐蓮。轉屈左足力士擋。並擒。踏右足雙掛入。疊退榻向前坐蓮。呈身雙扭。右足蹕。右手切。左手鈒。收立正。

Step forward with right leg, right hand *pian*. Step back while overlapping legs to assume the sitting on lotus posture facing the right side. Rotate into a left leg crouching stance, strong man thrust. Immediately *kim*. Step forward with right leg, *sang kwa lip*. Double step backward, overlapping to assume the sitting on lotus posture facing the front. Rise up, *sang liu*. *Tat* with the right leg. Right hand *chiat*, left hand *tueh*. Conclude. Stand erect

5

挑手前後法 – *Tioh Chiu Tsui Au Wat*
Flick Block, Front and Rear Method

踏右足右手挑。踏左足左手挑。退左足右手挑。翻後左手挑。踏右足挑。退右足左手挑。翻前右手挑。向左畔左手挑。翻右畔右手挑。向前左手挑。換右足右手轉破。收立正。

Step forward with right leg, right hand *tioh*. Step forward with left leg, left hand *tioh*. Step back with the left leg, right hand *tioh*. Turn to the rear, left hand *tioh*. Step forward with the right leg, *tioh*. Step back with right leg, left hand *tioh*. Turn to the front, right hand *tioh*. Face the left side, left hand *tioh*. Turn to the right, right hand *tioh*. Face the front, left hand *tioh*. Shift to the right leg, right hand *tsuan puah*. Conclude. Stand erect.

6

盖手四門法 – *Gai Chiu Se Mun Wat*
Scooping Hand, Four Doors Method

踏右足右手盖。翻後左手盖。翻前右手盖。向左畔左手盖。翻右畔右手盖。向前左手盖。並擒。換右足右手一拳。收立正。

Step forward with right leg, right hand *kay*. Turn to the rear, left hand *kay*. Turn to the front, left hand *kay*. Face the left side, left hand *kay*. Turn to the right side, right hand *kay*. Face the front, left hand *kay*. Immediately *kim*. Shift to the right leg, right hand *kun*. Conclude. Stand erect.

第五段
FIFTH LEVEL

1

雙開搨馬法 – *Sang Kai Tap Be Wat*
Double Low Block, Overlapping Step Method

閃搨右足雙開。閃搨左足雙開。換右足雙撟中。閃搨左足雙開。閃搨右足雙開。換左足雙撟中。閃搨右。閃搨左。換右足如法。收立正。

Evade overlapping with the right leg, *sang kai*. Evade with left lef overlapping step, *sang kai*. Shift to the right leg, *sang kiao* to the center. Evade with left lef overlapping step, *sang kai*. Evade with right leg overlapping step, *sang kai*. Shift to the left leg, *sang kiao* to the center. Evade with right leg overlapping step, then evade with left leg overlapping. Shift to the right leg and repeat the method (sequence). Conclude. Stand erect.

2

開擒前後屈 – *Kai Kim Tsui Au Kut*
Low Block, Grab Hand, Front and Rear Crouch

踏右足開。並擒。換左足開。並擒。踏右足撟。退屈左手開。呈身擒。踏右足右手刈。並托。左手擋。翻後左手擒。踏右足撟。退右足屈。翻前雙捲手。右足躂。左手切。右手釵。收立正。

Step forward with right leg, *kai*. Immediately *kim*. Shift to left leg, *kai*. Immediately *kim*. Step forward with right leg, *kiao*. Step back into a crouch, left hand *kai*. Rise up, *kim*. Step forward with right leg, *kua chat*. Immediately *tuh chiu*. Left hand *t'ng*. Turn to the rear, left hand *kim*. Step forward with the right leg, *kiao*. Step back with the right leg into a crouch. Turn to the front, *sang k'n chiu*. Right leg *tat*, left hand *chiat*, right hand *tueh*. Conclude. Stand erect.

3 ### 扯剪前後法 – *Chi Chian Tsui Au Wat*
Scissors Hold, Front and Rear Method

踏左足左手擒。右手切。換右足右手擒。左手切。換左手擒。踏右足雙扯剪。
並右挑。左切。翻後擒。踏右足雙扯剪。並右挑。左切。翻前擒。換右足右手
轉破。收立正。

Step forward with left leg, left hand *kim*. Right hand *chiat*. Shift to right leg, right hand *kim*. Left hand *chiat*. Shift to left leg, *kim*. Step forward with right leg, *sang chi chian*. Immediately right *tioh*. Left *chiat*. Turn to the rear, *kim*. Step forward with right leg, *sang chi chian*. Immediately right *tioh*. Left *chiat*. Turn to the front, *kim*. Shift to right leg, right hand *tsuan puah*. Conclude. Stand erect.

4 ### 雙盖鳳眼手 – *Sang Kay Hong Gan Chiu*
Double Scooping Hand, Phoenix-Eye Hand

踏右足雙盖。並鳳眼手。向左畔左手盖。右手刈節。翻右畔右手盖。左手刈
節。踏左足雙鈎。換右足雙摃。退寄和手擒。左手切。右手鳳眼。退寄招揚。
立正。

Step forward with right leg, immediately *hong gan chiu*. Face the left side, left hand *kay*. Right hand *kua chat*. Turn to the right side, right hand *kay*. left hand *kua chat*. Step forward with left leg, *sang kao*. Shift to right leg, *sang kong*. Step back to a hanging leg stance, *ho chiu kim*. Left hand *chiat*, right hand *hong gan*. Conclude. Stand erect.

5

指地閃屈法 – *Tsi Te Siam Kut Wat*
Pointing at the Ground, Evading Crouch Method

踏左足指地。並右手挑。左手挑。呈身右手切。並屈。呈身右手擒。進右屈雙
擒。進左屈雙擒。呈身退左足右手擒。收立正。

Step forward with the left leg, into a pointing-at-the-ground posture. Immediately right hand *tioh*, left hand *tioh*. Rise up, right hand *chiat*. Immediately crouch. Rise up, left hand *kim*. Step forward to the right in a crouch, *sang li*. Step forward to the left in a crouch, *sang li*. Rise up and step back with the left leg, right hand *kim*. Conclude. Stand erect.

6

落地折竹笋 – *Lok Teh At Sun Wat*
Falling to the Ground, Bending Bamboo Shoots

踏左足左手挑。並開。踏右足右手挑。並開。跳進屈右手擋。呈身雙卷手。跳
退抱牌。並屈右手擋。呈身雙卷手。左足躂。左手切。右手釼。收立正。

Step forward with left leg, left hand *tioh*. Immediately *kai*. Step forward with right leg, right hand *tioh*. Immediately *kai*. Jump forward into a crouch, right hand *t'ng*. Rise up, sang *k'n chiu*. Jump back, *po pai*. Immediately crouch, right hand *t'ng*. Rise up, sang *k'n chiu*. Left leg *tat*, left hand *chiat*, right hand *tueh*. Conclude. Stand erect.

1

盤手前後法 – *Pua Chiu Tsui Au Wat*
Coiling Hand, Front and Rear Method

閃右畔左手挑。右手切。左手切。閃左畔右手挑。左手切。右手切。換左足
擒。踏右足雙掛入。翻後擒。踏右足雙掛入。直進榻向前魁星手。並左手挑。
換右足右手轉破。收立正。

Evade to the right side, left hand *tioh*. Right hand chiat, left hand *chiat*. Evade to the left side, right hand *tioh*. Left hand *chiat*, right hand *chiat*. Shift to left leg, *kim*. Step forward with right leg, *sang kwa lip*. Turn to the rear, *kim*. Step forward with right leg, *sang kwa lip*. Step straight forward with overlapping step and facing the front in *kwi seng chiu* posture. Immediately left hand *tioh*. Shift to right leg, right hand *tsuan puah*. Conclude. Stand erect.

2

雙扭左右躂 – *Tat Sang Liu Zou Yu Tat*
Double Wrench, Left and Right Kick

踏右足向右角雙捲手。右足躂。踏左足向左角雙捲手。左足躂。退左足雙捲
手。右足躂。左手切。右手釸。收立正。

Step forward with right leg to the right corner, *sang k'n chiu*. Right leg *tat*. Step forward with left leg to the left corner, *sang k'n chiu*. Left leg *tat*. Step back with left leg, *sang k'n chiu*. Right leg *tat*, left hand *chiat*, right hand *tueh*. Conclude. Stand erect.

3

掃腳盤轉法 – *Sau Ka Pua Tsuan Wat*
Sweeping Leg, Coil and Rotate Method

踏右足貫中拳。脫手雙豎拳。向左掀。提右足掃向後平馬右手開。左手開。踏
左足掀。換右足掀。向左掀。提右足掃向前平馬右手開。左手開。踏左足掀。
換右足右手轉破。收立正。

Step forward with right leg, *kwan tiong kun. Tung chiu, sang kia kun*. Face the left, *hian*. Lift right leg and sweep to the rear into an even stance. Right hand *kai*, left hand *kai*. Step forward with left leg, *hian*. Shift to right leg, *hian*. Face the left, *hian*. Lift right leg and sweep to the front into an even stance. Right hand *kai*, left hand *kai*. Step forward with left leg, *hian*. Shift to the right leg, right hand *tsuan puah*. Conclude. Stand erect.

4

猴挑水法 – *Kao Tioh Sui Wat*
Monkey Flicking Water Method

踏左足平馬雙墜。吞手。側插。坐節。再吞手。側插。坐節。平馬左開。右
開。踏右足挑。換左足挑。換右手轉破。收立正。

Step forward with left leg into an even stance, *sang tui. Tun chiu. Chiak Cha*. Again *tun chiu, chaik cha. Che chat*. In an even stance, left *kai*, right *kai*. Step forward with right leg, *tioh*. Shift to left leg, *tioh*. Shift to right leg, right hand *tsuan puah*. Conclude. Stand erect.

5

參觀手法 – *Cham Guan Chiu Wat*
Observing Hand Method

閃右畔齊眉手。閃左閃右如法。進左足擒。切。進右足擒。切。退右足左手
挑。換右手轉破。收立正。

Evade to the right side, *che bi chiu*. Evade to the left and right, repeating the method. Step forward with left leg, *kim. Chiat.* Step forward right leg, *kim. Chiat.* Step back with right leg, left hand *tioh*. Shift to right leg, right hand *tsuan puah*. Conclude. Stand erect.

6

力士閃屈法 – *Lek Si Siam Kut Wat*
Strong Man, Evade and Crouch Method

向左屈雙擒。向右屈雙擒。呈身退右足左手擒。踏右足右手破。退榻向右坐
蓮。轉屈左足力士擋。進屈右手擋。呈身擒。換左足左手挑。換右足轉破。收
立正。

Facing the left, crouch. *Sang li.* Facing the right, crouch. *Sang li.* Rise up, stepping back with right leg, left hand *kim*. Step forward with right leg, right hand *puah*. Step backward with an overlapping step into a sitting on lotus posture facing the right. Rotate into a left leg crouch, strong-man-thrust. Forward right hand *t'ng*. Rise up, *kim*. Shift to left leg, left hand *tioh*. Shift to right leg, right hand *tsuan puah*. Conclude. Stand erect.

1

雙開左右法 – *Sang Kai Zou Yu Wat*
Double Down Block, Left and Right Method

進右足躂。並雙開。換左足躂。並雙開。閃榻右足雙開。閃榻左足雙開。換右
足雙搞。掇節。駿肸。換左足挑。換右手轉破。收立正。

Step forward, right leg *tat*. Immediately *sang kai*. Shift to left leg, *tat*. Immediately *sang kai*. Evade overlapping the right leg, *sang kai*. Evade overlapping the left leg, *sang kai*. Shift to right leg, *sang kiao, sang kwa chat, chun to*. Shift to left leg, left hand *tioh*. Shift to right leg, right hand *tsuan puah*. Conclude. Stand erect.

2

窵肩雙轉法 – *Tiao Kian Sang Tsuan Wat*
Side Shoulder Thrust, Double Rotate Method

閃平馬右手窵肩。閃左手窵肩。再閃如法。並右開。左開。踏左足擒。踏右足
雙掛入。翻後擒。踏右足三拳。翻前擒。換右手轉破。收立正。

Evade to an even stance, right hand *tiao kian*. Evade, left hand *tiao kian*. Again evade, repeating the same method (sequence). Immediately right evade, left evade. Step forward with left leg, *kim*. Step forward with right leg, *sang kwa lip*. Turn to the rear, *kim*. Step forward with right leg, *kun* three times alternating. Turn to the front, *kim*. Shift to right leg, right hand *tsuan puah*. Conclude. Stand erect.

3 閃馬開手法 – *Siam Be Kai Chiu Wat*
Evading Stance, Down Block Method

踏左足左手擒。踏右足葫蘆手。閃右手開。在馬向後閃左手開。再閃向前右手開。並和手掀。換左手挑。換右手轉破。收立正。

Step forward with left leg, left hand *kim*. Step forward with right leg, *o-lo chiu*. Evade, right hand *kai*. In the same stance, facing the rear, evade. Left hand *kai*. Again evade, facing the front. Right hand *kai*. Immediately *ho chiu hian*. Shift to left leg, left hand *tioh*. Shift to right leg, right hand *tsuan puah*. Conclude. Stand erect.

4 鈎搖雙批躂 – *Kao Yao Sang Pueh Tat*
Hook and Uppercut, Double Slapping Hand, Kick

踏左足左鈎右搖。踏右足雙批。平馬右鈎左搖。踏左足雙批。換右足雙批。並扭。右足躂。左手切。右手釵。收立正。

Step forward with left leg, left *kao*, right *yao*. Step forward with right leg, *sang peuh*. Even stance, right *kao*, left *yao*. Step forward with left leg, *sang peuh*. Shift to right leg, *sang peuh*. Immediately *liu*. Right leg *tat,* left hand *chiat*, right hand *tueh*. Conclude. Stand erect.

第七段
SEVENTH LEVEL

5

雙擋屈馬法 – *Sang T'ng Kut Be Wat*
Double Palm Thrust, Crouching Stance Method

踏右足雙擋。退右足抱盤接。退左足抱盤接。進抱牌。並屈右手開。呈身擒。退右足屈左手開。呈身擒。換右手轉破。收立正。

Step forward with right leg, *sang t'ng*. Step back with right leg, *po pua so*. Step back with left leg, *po pua so*. Step forward, *po pai*. Immediately crouch, right hand *kai*. Rise up, *kim*. Step back with right leg into a crouch, left hand *kai*. Rise up, *kim*. Shift to right leg, right hand *tsuan puah*. Conclude. Stand erect.

6

落地金鈎剪 – *Lo Teh Kim Kao Chien*
Falling to the Ground, Golden Hook Scissors

閃屈左畔。呈身雙卷手。右足躂。平馬左手擒。閃屈右畔。呈身左手擒。右手刈。踏右足雙鈎。扭進左足躂。並倒左側盤剪。反剪。鈎躂。進屈接。呈身扭。進抱牌。榻馬向後穿針。並倒剪。反剪盤左轉向後右手鞭。踏右足反馬搖。翻前踏右足撟。退寄左足羅漢手。左手挑。換右手轉破。收立正。

Evade into a left crouching stance. Rise up, *sang k'n chiu*. Tight leg *tat*. Rise up into even stance, left hand *kim*. Evade into a left crouching stance. Rise up, left hand *kim*. Right hand *kua chat*. Step forward with right leg, *sang kao*. *Liu*, then step forward and left leg *tat*. Immediately fall into a left side coiling scissor. Then reverse scissor and hook kick. Step forward into a crouch, and then *so*. Rise up, *liu*. Step forward, *po pai*. Overlapping step to the rear into a needle-piercing-sea-bottom posture. Falling scissors then reverse scissors. Coil to the left, facing rear, right hand *pian*. Step forward with right leg, *wan be yao*. Turn to the front and step forward with right leg, *kiao*. Step back into a left hanging leg stance, *lohan chiu*. Left hand *tioh*. Shift to right leg, right hand *tsuah pua*h. Conclude. Stand erect.

1

對摃雙轉法 – *Tui Kong Sang Tsuan Wat*
Opposing Hammer Strike, Double Rotate Method

踏右足右手摃。換左足左手摃。換右足撟。換左足撟。換右足對打。再換左手挑。換右手轉破。收立正。

Step forward with right leg, right hand *kong*. Shift to left leg, left hand *kong*. Shift to right leg, *kiao*. Shift to left leg, *kiao*. Shift to right leg, *dui da*. Again shift, left hand *tioh*. Shift to right leg, *tsuan puah*. Conclude. Stand erect.

2

挑開前後屈 – *Tioh Kai Tsui Au Kut*
Flick Block and Down Block, Front and Rear Crouch

踏右足挑。開。疊進右足挑。開。並擒。直進屈向後左手開。呈身擒。換右足挑。並開。疊進右足挑。開。疊退右足挑。開。並擒。直進屈向前左手開。呈身擒。換右手轉破。收立正。

Step forward with right leg, *tioh*, then *kai*. Double step forward, *tioh*, then *kai*. Immediately *kim*. Step straight forward into a crouch facing the rear, left hand *kai*. Rise up, *kim*. Shift to right leg, *tioh*. Immediately *kai*. Double step forward, *tioh*, then *kai*. Double step back, *tioh*, then *kai*. Immediately *kim*. Step straight forward into a crouch facing the front, left hand *kai*. Rise up, *kim*. Shift to right leg, right hand *tsuan puah*. Conclude. Stand erect.

3

挑屈擒之法 – *Tioh Kut Kim Ji Wat*
Flicking Block, Crouch and Grab Method

踏右足挑。並屈開。呈身擒。換左足挑。並屈開。呈身擒。踏右足撟。退寄左足羅漢手。並左手挑。換右足右手轉破。收立正。

Step forward with right leg, *tioh*. Immediately crouch, *kai*. Rise up, *kim*. Shift to left leg, *tioh*. Immediately crouch, *kai*. Rise up, *kim*. Step forward with right leg, *kiao*. Step back into a left hanging leg stance, *lohan chiu*. Immediately, left hand *tioh*. Shift to right leg, right hand *tsuan puah*. Conclude. Stand erect.

4

雙擒對閃法 – *Sang Kim Dui Siam Wat*
Double Grab, Opposing Evasion Method

踏右足擒。換左足擒。踏右足撟。退屈左手開。呈身擒。換右足對刈。並脫。踏左足右轉翻後右手擒。換左足擒。踏右足撟。退屈左手開。呈身擒。換右足對刈。並脫。跳向前至脫手。收立正。

Step forward with right leg, *kim*. Shift to left leg, *kim*. Step forward with right leg, *kiao*. Step back, into a crouch, *kai*. Rise up, *kim*. Shift to right leg, *dui kua*. Immediately *tung*. Step forward with left leg, rotating to the right to turn to the rear, right hand *kim*. Shift to left leg, *kim*. Step forward with right leg, *kiao*. Step back, into a crouch, *kai*. Rise up, *kim*. Shift to right leg, *dui kua*. Immediately *tung*. Jump to the front and repeat until *tung chiu*. Conclude. Stand erect.

5

擒撞對操法 – *Kim Chiend Dui Chao Wat*
Grab and Punch, Opposing Drill Method

踏右足右手一拳。左手擒。右手挑。左手開。再右手一拳如法。

Step forward with right leg, right hand *kun*. Left hand *kim*. Right hand *tioh*. Left hand *kai*. Repeat the method (sequence), starting with the right hand.

6

虎仔神腰法 – *Ho A Chun Kiu Wat*
Tiger Stretching the Waist Method

踏右角雙挨。踏左雙挨。踏右足鳳尾彩。摔刜。雙挑。坐節。扭雙擋。再扭右手擋。左手擋。右手擋。退右足左手挑。換右足轉破。收立正。

Step to the right corner, *sang so*. Step to the left corner, *sang so*. Step forward with the right leg, *hong be tsai*. *Sut to*. *Sang tioh*. *Che Chat*. *Liu*. *Sang t'ng*. Repeat *liu,* right hand *t'ng*, left hand *t'ng*, and right hand *t'ng*. Step back with the right leg, left hand *tioh*. Shift to right leg, *tsuan puah*. Conclude. Stand erect.

Volume 5
第五編

NATIONAL TECHNIQUES, SIX ARTS METHODS
國技六藝法

WEAPONS OF NGO CHO KUN

Beng Kiam students demonstrating paired weapons form, (1960s).

Editor's Note: *Although Ngo Cho Kun is a southern system and has many weapon forms, its two main weapons are the sang te pi ("double rotating whips" or "iron rulers") and the kun or "staff." In this book, Yu Chiok Sam presented six weapons: the spear, single broadsword, double stright swords, double rotating whips, pole and the sky halberd. However, for whatever reason, he omited mention of the Kwan dao, horse cutter, iron crutches, tri-section staff, single saber, double broadswords, butterfly sword and round shield, and others.*

In traditional Chinese kung-fu the weapons forms and techniques are oftentimes attributed to famous generals or dieties and passed down unchanged for generations. In Ngo Cho Kun, the situation is quite different. The main point of interest is that while all lineages of Ngo Cho Kun trace back to one of the "10 Tigers" or senior students of Chua Giok Beng, they all have different weapon forms. What's more interesting is that many of the weapon forms hold the same name, but their coreography is completely different. Perhaps not all masters learned the forms and so created new sequences under the original names so as not to appear to be of lesser knowledge. We may never know, as reasons for this have been lost in time.

<table>
<tr><td>

22

</td><td>

齊眉棍 - Che Bi Kun
EYEBROW HEIGHT STAFF

</td></tr>
</table>

Alfredo Yu poses with the eyebrow height staff

一節 十四法 - 1ST SECTION, 14 METHODS

立正。踏右足破。平馬掃。踏左角橋。退寄押。疊進截。退右足向後過攔。
旋螺跳向後破。跳向前過攔。踏左角斬。疊進過攔。疊退截。走馬向右押上。
走馬向左斬上。退寄押下。疊退收截。立正。

Stand erect. Step forward with right leg, *puah*. Assume an even stance, *sao*. Step forward to the left corner, *kiao*. Step back into hanging leg stance, *kap*. Double step forward, *chà*. Step back with right leg to face the rear, *ge*. Whirlwind jump facing the rear, *puah*. Jump to face the front, *ge*. Step forward to the left corner, *cham*. Double step forward, *ge*. Double step back, *chà*. Walk toward the right, *kap* upward. Walk toward the left, *cham* upward. Step back to a hanging leg stance, *kap* downward. Double step back to conclude with *chà*. Stand erect.

二節十六法 – 2ND SECTION, 16 METHODS

踏右足破。換左足掃。換右足橋。平馬過攔。轉斬左。疊進挑。摔。箭。翻後箭。平馬斬。踏右足戴插。跳向前過攔。旋螺跳向前破。跳向後過攔。搨轉向前斬。退寄押。疊退收截。

Step forward with right leg, *puah*. Shift to left leg, *sao*. Shift to right leg, *kiao*. Assume an even stance, *ge*. Rotating *cham*, left. Double step forward, *tioh*. *Sut. Tsi.* Turn to the rear, *tsi*. Assume an even stance, *cham*. Step forward with *dai cha*. Jump to face front, *ge*. Whirlwind jump facing the front, *puah*. Jump to face rear, *ge*. Overlapping step to rotate facing front, *cham*. Step back to a hanging leg stance, *kap* downward. Double step back to conclude with *chà*.

三節 十八法 – 3RD SECTION, 18 METHODS

踏右足破。平馬掃。踏左角斬。踏右角戴。踏左角戴。踏右足戴中。跳向後過攔。旋螺跳向後破。跳向前過攔。踏左角斬。踏右足反斬。並破。直進箭。跳退平馬箭左。踏右足箭。平馬橋。退寄押。直進箭。收截。

Step forward with right leg, *puah*. Assume an even stance, *sao*. Step forward to left corner, *cham*. Step forward to right corner, *ti*. Step forward to left corner, *ti*. Step forward with right leg, *ti* to the center. Jump to face rear, *ge*. Whirlwind jump to face rear, *puah*. Jump to face front, *ge*. Step to the left corner, *cham*. Step with the right foot, *wan cham*. Immediately *puah*. Step straight forward, *tsi*. Jump to the rear in an even stance, *tsi* to the left. Step forward with right leg, *tsi*. Assume an even stance, *kiao*. Step back to a hanging leg stance, *kap*. Step straight forward, *tsi*. Conclude with *chà*.

Willy Key demonstrates 7-foot Pole

四節 二十法 – 4TH SECTION, 20 METHODS

踏右足破。退右足向後過攔。搨轉向前斬。搨轉向右畔過攔。搨轉向左畔斬。退寄押。疊退截。走馬屈押右。屈斬左。踏右足過攔。旋螺跳向前破。跳向後過攔。踏左角截。踏右足過攔。翻前斬。踏右足反手斬。並破。直進箭。跳退平馬橋。踏右足挑。收截。

Step forward with right leg, *puah*. Step back with right leg to face the rear, *ge*. Step overlapping to rotate facing the front, *cham*. Step overlapping to rotate facing the right side, *ge*. Step overlapping to rotate facing the left side, *cham*. Step back to a hanging leg stance, *kap*. Double step back, *chà*. Walking step into a crouch, *kap* to the right. Crouch and cham to the left. Step forward with right leg, *ge*. Whirlwind jump to face the front, *puah*. Jump to face rear, *ge*. Step to the left corner, *chà*. Step with right leg, *ge*. Turn to the front, *cham*. Step forward with right leg, reverse hand *cham*. Immediately *puah*. Step straight forward, *tsi*. Jump back to an even stance, *kiao*. Step forward with right leg, *tioh*. Conclude with *chà*.

五節 廿二法 – 5TH SECTION, 22 METHODS

踏右足破。退右足掃。退左足橋。並曲。進截。退寄捲。直進箭。跳進點。掇。箭。退搨橫馬押。換平馬截。退寄押。踏左足斬。疊進過攔。旋螺跳向前破。跳向後過攔。搨轉向前斬。閃左畔齊眉手。閃右畔齊眉手。退寄押。並箭。收截。

Step forward with right leg, *puah*. Step back with right leg, *sao*. Step back with left leg, kiao. Immediately *aw*. Step forward, *chà*. Step back to a hanging leg stance, *k'n*. Step straight forward, *tsi*. Jump forward, *tiam*. *Kwa*. *Tsi*. Overlapping step back to a horizontal stance, *kap*. Shift to an even stance, *chà*. Step back to a hanging leg stance, *kap*. Step forward with left leg, *cham*. Double step forward, *ge*. Whirlwind jump to face front, *puah*. Jump to face rear, *ge*. Step overlapping to rotate to front, *cham*. Evade to the left side, *che bi chiu*. Evade to the right side, *che bi chiu*. Step back to a hanging leg stance, *kap*. Immediately *tsi*. Conclude with *chà*.

六節 二四法 – 6TH SECTION, 24 METHODS

進點左。點右平馬橋。踏右足挑。摔。箭。跳退平馬掃。踏左角橋。踏右足曲。截。捲。箭。翻後箭。退寄押。平馬橋。踏左角截。踏右足過攔。旋螺跳向後破。跳向前過攔。踏左足斬。踏右足反手斬。踏左角戴。踏右足過攔。反手箭。收截。

Step forward, *tiam* left. *Tiam* right, then assume an even stance, *kiao*. Step forward with right leg, *tioh*. *Sut*. *Tsi*. Jump back to an even stance, *sao*. Step forward to the left corner, *kiao*. Step forward with right leg, *aw*. *Chà*. *K'n*. *Tsi*. Turn to the rear, *tsi*. Step back to a hanging leg stance, *kap*. Assume an even stance, *kiao*. Step to the left corner, *chà*. Step forward with right leg, *ge*. Whirlwind jump to face the rear, *puah*. Jump to face the front, *ge*. Step forward with lef leg, *cham*. Step forward with right leg, reverse hand *cham*. Step to the left corner, *ti* Step forward with right leg, *ge*. Reverse hand *tsi*. Conclude with *chà*.

七節 二六法 – 7TH SECTION, 26 METHODS

踏右足破。平馬掃。踏左角橋。踏右足掃。並破。平馬屈右攔。屈斬左。疊進過攔。旋螺跳向前破。跳向後過攔。踏左角斬。踏右足戴。跳向前過攔。踏左角斬。退寄押。進截。並挑。摔。箭。跳退平馬橋。並曲。進截。過挑右。過截左。退寄捲。並箭。收截。

Step forward with right leg, *puah*. Assume an even stance, *sao*. Step to left corner, *kiao*. Step forward with right leg, *sao*. Immediately *puah*. Assume an even stance, crouching with *ge* on the right. Crouch with *cham* on the left. Double step forward, *ge*. Whirlwind jump to face front, *puah*. Jump to face rear, *ge*. Step to the left corner, *cham*. Step forward with right leg, *ti*. Jump to face front, *ge*. Step to the left corner, *cham*. Step back to hanging leg stance, *kap*. Step forward, *chà*. Immediately *tioh*. *Sut*. *Tsi*. Jump back to assume an even stance, *kiao*. Immediately *aw*. Step forward, *chà*. Crossing *tioh* to the right. Crossing *chà* to the left. Step back to a hanging leg stance, *k'n*. Immediately *tsi*. Conclude with *chà*.

八節 二八法 – 8TH SECTION, 28 METHODS

進點左。點右。進截。退押。並曲。進插。挑。摔。箭。翻後箭。平馬斬。踏右足過攔。旋螺跳向後破。跳向前過攔。疊進反手箭。跳退平馬掃。踏左角橋。橫馬押。走馬掃。平馬斬。踏左足過攔。搨轉向左畔斬。搨轉向右畔過攔。搨轉向前斬。退寄押。疊退截。捲。箭。收截。

Step forward, *tiam* to the left. *Tiam* to the right. Step forward, *chà*. Step back, *kap*. Immediately *aw* Step forward, *cha*. *Tioh*. *Sut*. *Tsi*. Turn to the rear, *tsi*. Assume an even stance, *cham*. Step forward with right leg, *ge*. Whirlwind jump facing rear, *puah*. Jump to face front, *ge*. Double step forward, reverse hand *tsi*. Jump back to an even stance, *sao*. Step to the left corner, *kiao*. Assume a horizontal stance, *kap*. Walking step, *sao*. Assume an even stance, *cham*. Step forward with left leg, *ge*. Step overlapping to rotate with *cham*, facing the left side. Step overlapping to rotate with *ge*, facing the right side. Step overlapping to rotate with *cham*, facing the front. Step back into a hanging leg stance, *kap*. Double step back, *chà*. *K'n*. *Tsi*. Conclude with *chà*.

Alex Co demonstrating eyebrow-height staff in the late 1960s.

<h1>棍術練習法</h1>
<h1>STAFF PRACTICE METHOD</h1>

<h1>即仙人指路</h1>
<h1>"IMMORTAL POINTING THE WAY"</h1>

立正。踏右馬破。閃右角掃。踏左角斬。踏右足掃中。並破。直進箭。踏左足平馬截。退寄押下。直進箭。翻後箭。閃左角斬。踏右足掃中。並破。直進箭。翻後箭。閃左角斬。疊進右足過攔。直進反手箭。退右足掃。退左足橋。並曲右。直進截。退寄捲。進中箭。收立正。

Stand erect. Step forward to a right stance, *puah*. Evade to the right corner, *sao*. Step to the left corner, *cham*. Step forward with right leg, *sao* to the center. Immediately *puah*. Step straight forward, *tsi*. Step forward with left leg to an even stance, *chà*. Step back to a hanging leg stance, kap downward. Step straight forward, *tsi*. Turn to the rear, *tsi*. Evade to left corner, *cham*. Step forward with right leg, *sao* to the center. Immediately *puah*. Step straight forward, *tsi*. Turn to the rear, *tsi*. Evade to the left corner, *cham*. Double step forward, reverse hand *tsi*. Step back with right leg, *sao*. Step back with left leg, *kiao*. Immediately *aw* to the right. Step straight forward, *chà*. Step back to a hanging leg stance, *k'n*. Step forward, *tsi* to the center. Conclude, standing erect.

William Uy demonstrates 7-foot Pole

棍術練習法
STAFF PRACTICE METHOD

即白蛇捲地
"WHITE SNAKE COILED ON THE GROUND"

進點左。進點右。進截中。退寄押。疊退曲。進插下。疊進挑。退寄押。摔直
進箭。跳退平馬掃。平馬撟。橫馬押。走馬掃。平馬斬。疊進右足過攔。旋螺
跳向前破。跳向後過攔。踏左角斬。踏右足戴插。退寄捲。直進箭。翻前箭。
閃左角斬。踏右足反手斬。踏左角斬。踏右足曲。直進點左。並掇右。進中
箭。退塌橫馬押下。換平馬截。退寄押。 踏左足平馬截上。走馬屈押右。轉斬
左。退寄押下。疊退截。收立正。

Step forward, *tiam* to the left. Step forward, *tiam* to the right. Step forward, *chà* to the center. Step back to a hanging leg stance, *kap*. Double step back, *aw*. Step forward, *cha* downward. Double step forward, *tioh*. Step back to a hanging leg stance, *kap*. *Sut*, then step straight forward, *tsi*. Jump back to an even leg stance, *sao*. Assume an even stance, *kiao*. Assume a horizontal stance, *kap*. Walking step, *sao*. Assume an even stance, *cham*. Double step forward, starting with right leg, *ge*. Whirlwind jump facing front, *puah*. Jump to face rear, *ge*. Step to the left corner, *cham*. Step forward with right leg, *ti cha*. Step back to a hanging leg stance, *k'n*. Step straight forward, *tsi*. Turn to the front, *tsi*. Evade to the left corner, *cham*. Step forward with right leg, reverse hand *cham*. Step to the left corner, *cham*. Step forward with right leg, *aw*. Step straight forward, *tiam* to the left. Immediately *kwa* to the right. Step forward, *tsi* to the center. Step back overlapping to a horizontal stance, *kap* downward. Shift to an even stance, *chà*. Step back to a hanging leg stance, *kap*. Step forward with left leg to an even stance, *chà* upward. Walking step into a crouching stance, *kap* to the right. Rotating *cham* to the left. Step back to a hanging leg stance, *kap* downward. Double step back, *chà*. Conclude, standing erect.

棍術練習法
STAFF PRACTICE METHOD

即青龍卷水
"GREEN DRAGON COILED IN THE WATER"

踏右足破。換左足掃右。換右足橋左。平馬掃。平馬橋。踏右足掃中。並破。
退右足向後過攔。塌轉向左畔。踏左足平馬斬。塌轉向右畔。右足過攔。塌轉
向中。踏左足斬。閃右畔。吊右足。押下。閃左畔。吊左足。反手押下。退寄
押。平馬斬。疊進右足挑。退寄摔。進中箭。翻前箭。閃角斬。踏右角戴插
右。踏左角戴插左。踏右足反手斬。進橋中。閃塌右畔押下。閃塌左畔截。平
馬屈押右。轉斬左。踏右足過攔。旋螺跳向前破。跳向後過攔。塌轉向前斬。
塌轉向右押上。塌轉向左斬上。塌進中過攔。旋螺跳向前破。收立正。

Step forward with right leg, *puah*. Shift to left leg, *sao* to the right. Shift to right leg, *kaio* to the left. Assume an even stance, *sao*. Still in an even stance, *kiao*. Step forward with right leg, *sao* to the center. Immediately *puah*. Step back with right leg to face rear, *ge*. Step overlapping to face the left side, stepping forward with left leg into an even stance, *cham*. Step overlapping to face the right side, *ge*. Step overlapping to face the center, stepping forward with left leg, *cham*. Evade to the right side, hanging the right leg, *kap* downward. Evade to the left side, hanging the left leg, reverse hand *kap* downward. Step back into a hanging leg stance, *kap*. Assume an even stance, *cham*. Double step forward, starting with right leg, *tioh*. Step back into a hanging leg stance, *sut*. Step forward, *tsi* to the center. Turn to the front, *tsi*. Evade to the corner, *cham*. Step to the right corner, *cha* to the right. Step to the left corner, *cha* to the left. Step forward with right leg, reverse hand *cham*. Step forward, *kiao* to the center. Evade overlapping to the right side, *kap* downward. Evade overlapping to the left side, *chà*. Assume an even stance and then crouch, *kap* to the right. Rotating *cham* to the left. Step forward with right leg, *ge*. Whirlwind jump to face front, *puah*. Jump to face rear, *ge*. Step overlapping to face the front, *cham*. Step overlapping to face the right, *kap* upward. Step overlapping to face the left, *cham* upward. Step forward overlapping to the center, *ge*. Whirlwind jump to face the front, *puah*. Conclude, standing erect.

棍術對操法
STAFF OPPOSING PRACTICE METHOD

上機	Side A	下機	Side B
踏右足對破上	Step forward with right leg, opposing *puah* upward.	踏右足對破	Step forward with right leg, opposing *puah*.
平馬掃	Assume an even stance, *sao*.	平馬掃	Assume an even stance, *sao*.
平馬橋	Assume an even stance, *kiao*.	平馬橋	Assume an even stance, *kiao*.
反打右	*Wan ta* to the right.	反打右	Wan *ta* to the right.
並打左	Immediately *ta* to the left.	並打左	Immediately *ta* to the left.
退右足掃	Step back with right leg, *sao*.	踏左足掃	Step forward with left leg, *sao*.
退左足橋	Step back with left leg, *kiao*.	踏右足橋	Step right leg forward, *kiao*.
並曲右	Immediately *aw* to the right.	退右足掃	Step back with right leg, *sao*.
踏左足掃	Step forward with left leg, *sao*.	退足左橋	Step back with left leg, *kiao*.
踏右足橋	Step forward with right leg, *kiao*.	並曲右	Immediately *aw* to the right.
跳退曲右	Jump back, *aw* to the right.	跳進箭上	Jump forward, *tsi* upward.
跳進箭上	Jump forward, *tsi* upward.	跳退曲右	Jump back, *aw* to the right.
跳退戴插	Jump back, *ti* cha.	疊進過攔	Double step forward, *ge*.
疊進右足對破	Double step forward, starting with right leg, opposing *puah*.	旋螺跳向前對破	Whirlwind jump to face front, opposing *puah*.
並截	Immediately *chà*.	並截	Immediately *chà*.
疊進過攔	Double step forward, *ge*.	跳退戴插	Jump back, *ti* cha.
旋螺跳向前對破	Whirlwind jump to face front, opposing *puah*.	疊進右足對破	Double step forward, starting with right leg, opposing *puah*.
平馬屈斬左	Assume an even stance, then crouch and *cham* to the left	跳高	Jump over the attack.
屈斬右	Crouching, *cham* to the right.	再跳高	Again, Jump over the attack.
退左足對破	Step back with left leg, opposing *puah*.	踏右足對破	Step forward with right leg, opposing *puah*.
跳高	Jump over the attack.	平馬屈斬左	Assume an even stance, then crouch and *cham* to the left.
再跳高	Again, jump over the attack.	屈斬右	Crouching, *cham* to the right.
踏右足對破	Step forward with right leg, opposing *puah*.	退左足對破	Step back with left leg, opposing *puah*.
並截	Immediately *chà*.	並截	Immediately *chà*.
收立正	Conclude by standing erect.	收立正	Conclude by standing erect.

23

單刀法 - Tan To
SINGLE SABER METHOD

Benito Tan posing with tan-to

單刀第一節 – SINGLE SABER – 1ST SECTION

踏右足請。踏左角斬。踏右足開。疊退破。疊進箭。疊退箭。走馬屈押右。屈斬左。踏右足戴。閃截。並開。旋螺跳向前破。跳向後開。踏左足斬。踏右足開。楊轉向前斬。換右足躂。並開。疊退破。收立正。

Step forward with right leg and perform the salutation. Step to the left corner, *cham*. Step forward with right leg, *kai*. Double step back, *puah*. Double step forward, *tsi*. Double step backward, *tsi*. Walking step into a crouch, *kap* to the right. Still crouching, *cham* to the left. Step forward with right leg, *ti*. Evade, *chà*. Immediately *kai*. Whirlwind jump facing front, *puah*. Jump to face rear, *kai*. Step forward with left leg, *cham*. Step forward with right leg, *kai*. Overlapping step, then rotate to face front, *cham*. Shift to right leg, *tat*. Immediately *kai*. Double step backward, *puah*. Conclude by standing erect.

單刀第二節 – SINGLE SABER– 2ND SECTION

踏右足請。踏左足斬。踏右足開。疊退破。平馬屈押右。屈斬左。踏右足開。旋螺跳向前破。跳向後開。踏左足斬。踏右足開。疊退破。跳向前開。踏左足斬。踏右足戴。閃截。並開。疊退破。收立正。

Step forward with right leg and perform the salutation. Step forward with left leg, *cham*. Step forward with right leg, *kai*. Double step back, *puah*. Assume an even stance, then crounch with downward *kap*. Still crouching, *cham* to the left. Step forward with right leg, *kai*. Whirlwind jump facing front, *puah*. Jump to face rear, *kai*. Step forward with left leg, *cham*. Step forward with right leg, *kai*. Double step back, *puah*. Jump to face front, *kai*. Step forward with left leg, *cham*. Step forward with right leg, *ti*. Evade, *chà*. Immediately *kai*. Double step backward, *puah*. Conclude by standing erect.

單刀第三節 - SINGLE SABER– 3RD SECTION

踏右足請。踏左足斬。踏右足開。榻轉向左畔斬上。榻轉向右畔押上。榻轉向前斬。榻轉向後開。榻轉向前斬。換右足蹳。並開。疊退破。走馬押右。走馬斬左。疊進中開。旋螺跳向前破。跳向後開。疊進橋。退右足向前開弓。並破。收立正。

Step forward with right leg and perform the salutation. Step forward with left leg, *cham*. Step forward with right leg, *kai*. Overlapping step then rotate to face the left side, *cham* upward. Overlapping step then rotate to face the right side, *kap* upward. Step overlapping then rotate to face front, *cham*. Overlapping step then rotate to face rear, *kai*. Overlapping step then rotate to face front, *cham*. Shift to right leg, *tat*. Immediately *kai*. Double step backward, *puah*. Walking step, *kap* to the right. Walking step, *cham* to the left. Double step forward to center, *kai*. Whirlwind jump facing front, *puah*. Jump to face rear, *kai*. Double step forward, *kiao*. Step back with right leg to face front, *kwi kieng*. Immediately *puah*. Conclude by standing erect.

單刀第四節 – SINGLE SABER– 4TH SECTION

踏右足請。踏左足斬。踏右足開。並破。退右足向後開弓。旋螺跳向後破。平
馬屈押右。屈斬左。踏右足開。榻轉向前斬。榻轉向右畔開。榻轉向左畔斬。
疊進中開。疊退破。平馬開。平馬斬。踏右足開。並破。收。

Step forward with right leg and perform the salutation. Step forward with left leg, *cham*.
Step forward with right leg, *kai*. Immediately *puah*. Step back with right leg to face rear,
kwi kieng. Whirlwind jump facing rear, *puah*. Assume an even stance, then crouch and *kap*
to the right. Still crouching, *cham* to the left. Step forward with right leg, *kai*. Step overlapping then rotate to face front, *cham*. Overlapping step then rotate to face the right side,
kai. Overlapping step then rotate to face the left side, *cham*. Double step forward to center,
kai. Double step back, *puah*. Assume an even stance, *kai*. Still in an even stance, *cham*. Step
forward with right leg, *kai*. Immediately *puah*. Conclude.

單刀第五節 – SINGLE SABER– 5TH SECTION

踏右足請。踏左足斬。踏右足開。並破。榻馬開弓。翻前斬。翻後開。踏左足
斬。榻轉向前開。踏左角斬。踏右足戴。閃截。並開。旋螺跳向前破。閃榻右
畔右手開。閃榻左畔右手截。換左足右手箭。換右足破。收立正。

Step forward with right leg and perform the salutation. Step forward with left leg, *cham*.
Step forward with right leg, *kai*. Immediately *puah*. Step overlapping, *kwi kieng*. Turn to
the front, *cham*. Turn to the rear, *kai*. Step forward with left leg, *cham*. Overlapping step,
then rotate to face front, *kai*. Step to the left corner, *cham*. Step forward with right leg, *ti*.
Evade, chà. Immediately *kai*. Whirlwind jump facing front, *puah*. Evade with overlapping
step to the right side, right hand *kai*. Evade with overlapping step to the left side, right
hand chà. Shift to left leg, right hand *tsi*. Shift to right leg, *puah*. Conclude by standing
erect.

單刀第六節 – SINGLE SABER – 6TH SECTION

踏右足請。踏左足斬。榻轉向後開。榻轉向左畔斬。榻轉向右畔押。榻轉向中斬。換右足。並開躂。疊退破。跳向前開。並破。走馬押右。走馬斬左。疊進中開。旋螺跳向前破疊進箭。平馬斬。踏右足開。疊退破。收立正。

Step forward with right leg and perform the salutation. Step forward with left leg, *cham*. Overlapping step to the left side, cham. Overlapping step and then rotate to face the right side, *kap*. Overlapping step and then rotate to face the center, *cham*. Shift right leg, Immediately *kai* and *tat*. Double step backward, *puah*. Jump to face front, *kai*. Immediately *puah*. Walking step, *kap* to the right. Walking step, *cham* to the left. Double step forward to center, *kai*. Whirlwind jump facing front, *puah*. Double step forward, *tsi*. Assume an even stance, *cham*. Step forward with right leg, *kai*. Double step backward, *puah*. Conclude by standing erect.

單刀第七節 – SINGLE SABER– 7TH SECTION

踏右足請。踏左足斬。踏右足開。旋螺跳向前破。走馬押右。走馬斬左。退中開。疊退破。跳退開。疊進橋。疊進破。退右足閃左手開。退左足扭右足躂。並開。翻前屈。呈轉破。翻後斬。收立正。

Step forward with right leg and perform the salutation. Step forward with left leg, *cham*. Step forward with right leg, *kai*. Whirlwind jump facing front, *puah*. Walking step, *kap* to the right. Walking step, *cham* to the left. Step back to center, *kai*. Double step backward, *puah*. Jump back, *kai*. Double step forward, *kiao*. Double step forward, *puah*. Step back with right leg, evading, left hand *kai*. Step back with left leg, *liu*, right leg *tat*. Immediately *kai*. Turn to rear, crouching. Rise up, rotating, *puah*. Turn to rear, *cham*. Conclude by standing erect.

單刀第八節 – SINGLE SABER – 8TH SECTION

踏右足請。踏左足斬。退左足齊眉手。翻後斬。退左足齊眉手。翻前斬。踏右足戴。閃截。並開。旋螺跳向前破。跳向後開。踏左足斬。榻轉向前開。榻轉向左畔斬。榻轉向右畔押。榻轉向前斬。換右足蹕。並開。疊退破。收。

Step forward with right leg and perform the salutation. Step forward with left leg, *cham*. Step back with left leg, *che bi chiu*. Turn to the rear, *cham*. Step back with left leg, *che bi chiu*. Turn to the front, *cham*. Step forward with right leg, *ti*. Evade, *chà*. Immediately *kai*. Whirlwind jump facing front, *puah*. Jump to face rear, *kai*. Step forward with left leg, *cham*. Step overlapping then rotate to face front, *kai*. Step overlapping then rotate to face the left side, *cham*. Step overlapping then rotate to face the right side, *kap*. Step overlapping then rotate to face front, *cham*. Shift to right leg, *tat*. Immediately *kai*. Double step backward, *puah*. Conclude.

Mark V. Wiley posing with broadsword

Bonifacio Lim posing with broadsword

單刀練習法
SINGLE SABER PRACTICE METHOD

郎英雄獨立
"HERO STANDS INDEPENDENTLY"

榻進請。退寄請。退右足斬。踏右角押上。踏左角打上。踏右足開。直進破。退右足向後開弓。旋螺跳向後破。跳向前開。直進破。榻馬開弓。翻前斬。翻後開。踏左足斬。榻轉向前開。踏左角斬。踏右足戴。閃截。並開。疊退破。走馬押右。走馬斬左。退寄開。疊退破。跳退開。疊進撟。疊進破。退閃左手開。退左足扭右足蹴。並開。疊退破。平馬屈押右。屈斬左。踏右足開。榻轉向後斬。翻榻向前屈。呈轉破。搨進請。退寄請。平馬抽刀。收立正。

Step forward with an overlapping and perform the salutation. Step back to a hanging leg stance and perform the salutation. Step back with right leg, *cham*. Step to the right corner, *kap* upward. Step to the left corner, *ta* upward. Step forward with right leg, *kai*. Step straight forward, *puah*. Step back with right leg facing rear, *kwi kieng*. Whirlwind jump facing rear, *puah*. Jump to face front, *kai*. Step straight forward, *puah*. Step overlapping, *kwi kieng*. Turn to the front, *cham*. Turn to the rear, *kai*. Step forward with left leg, *cham*. Overlapping step forward, then rotate to face front, *kai*. Step to the left corner, *cham*. Step forward with right leg, *ti*. Evade, *chà*. Immediately *kai*. Double step backward, *puah*. Walking step, *kap* to the right. Walking step, *cham* to the left. Step back to a hanging leg stance, *kai*. Double step backward, *puah*. Jump back, *kai*. Double step forward, *kiao*. Double step forward, *puah*. Step back, evading, left hand *kai*. Step back with left leg, *liu*, then right leg kick. Immediately *kai*. Double step backward, *puah*. Assume an even stance, then crouch, *kap* to the right. Still crouching, *cham* to the left. Step forward with right leg, *kai*. Overlapping step, then rotate to face rear, *cham*. Turn with overlapping step to face the front in a crouch. Rise up, rotating, *puah*. Forward overlapping step to perform the saluation. Step back to a hanging leg stance and perform the salutation. Assume an even stance, put away the saber. Conclude by standing erect.

<table>
<tr><td>

24

</td><td>

雙劍術 - Sang Teh Kiam
DOUBLE STRAIGHT SWORD METHOD

</td></tr>
</table>

雙劍第一節 – DOUBLE STRAIGHT SWORD – 1ST SECTION

踏右足戴。踏左足雙斬。踏右角押。切。踏左角押。切。退右手開。退左手開。踏右足右手破。退馬屈右手斬。踏右足戴。並刈。右手挑。左手切。榻馬開弓。翻前雙轉。翻後雙轉。踏左足左手開。右手切。榻轉向前雙批。疊退雙破。收立正。

Step forward with right leg, *ti*. Step forward with left leg, *sang cham*. Step to the right corner, *kap*. *Chiat*. Step to the left corner, *kap*. *Chiat*. Step back, right hand *kai*. Step back, left hand *kai*. Step forward with right leg, right hand *puah*. Step back into a crouching stance, right hand *cham*. Step forward with right leg, *ti*. Immediately *kua*. *Tioh* with the right hand, *chiat* with the left hand. Step overlapping, *kwi kieng*. Turn to the front, *sang tsuan*. Turn to the rear, *sang tsuan*. Step forward with left leg, left hand *kai*. Right hand *chiat*. Overlapping step, then rotate to front, *sang pueh*. Double step back, *sang puah*. Conclude by standing erect.

雙劍第二節 – DOUBLE STRAIGHT SWORD – 2ND SECTION

踏右足戴。踏左足雙斬。踏右足雙批。旋螺跳向前雙破。跳向後雙批。退馬屈。右手斬。踏右足戴。並刈。右手挑。左手切。榻馬開弓。翻向後雙轉。翻向前雙轉。踏左足開。換右足蹤。切。並雙開。翻後左足蹤。並雙開。踏右足開。切。榻轉向前雙批。換右足雙批。疊退雙破。收立正。

Step forward with right leg, *ti*. Step forward with left leg, *sang cham*. Step forward with right leg, *sang pueh*. Whirlwind jump facing front, *sang puah*. Jump to face rear, *sang pueh*. Step back into a crouching stance, right hand *cham*. Step forward with right leg, *ti*. Immediately *kua*. *Tioh* with the right hand, *chiat* with the left hand. Overlapping step, *kwi kieng*. Turn to the front, *sang tsuan*. Turn to the rear, *sang tsuan*. Step forward with left leg, left hand *kai*. Shift to right leg, *tat*. *Chiat*. Immediately *sang kai*. Turn to the rear, left leg *tat*. Immediately *sang kai*. Step forward with right leg, *kai*. *Chiat*. Step overlapping, then rotate to face front, *sang pueh*. Shift to the right leg, *sang pueh*. Double step back, *sang puah*. Conclude by standing erect.

雙劍第三節 – DOUBLE STRAIGHT SWORDS – 3RD SECTION

踏右足戴。踏左足雙斬。踏右足雙批。榻轉向後雙批。榻轉向前雙批。榻轉向左畔雙批。榻轉向右畔雙批。向前左手開。踏右足右手破。退馬屈。右手斬。踏右足戴。並刈。右手挑。左手切。榻馬開弓。翻向前雙轉。踏右足雙批。疊退雙破。收。

Step forward with right leg, *ti*. Step forward with left leg, *sang cham*. Step forward with right leg, *sang pueh*. Step overlapping, then rotate to face rear, *sang pueh*. Step overlapping, then rotate to face front, *sang pueh*. Step overlapping, then rotate to face the left side, *sang pueh*. Overlapping step, then rotate to face the right side, *sang pueh*. Face the front, left hand *kai*. Step forward with right leg, right hand *puah*. Step back into a crouch. Right hand *cham*. Step forward with right leg, *ti*. Immediately *kua*. Right hand *tioh*. Left hand *chiat*. Overlapping step, *kwi kieng*. Turn to face the front, *sang tsuan*. Step forward with right leg, *sang pueh*. Double step back, *sang puah*. Conclude.

雙劍第四節 – DOUBLE STRAIGHT SWORDS – 4TH SECTION

踏右足戴。踏左足雙斬。進右足躂。並雙開。退右足向右。向後。向左。向前雙開弓。退榻馬向前開弓。翻向前雙轉。翻向後雙轉。踏左足左手開。右手切。榻轉向前右手開。左手切。退右足齊眉手。進左角押。切。進右角押。切。退左手開。踏右足雙批。疊退雙破。收立正。

Step forward with right leg, *ti*. Step forward with left leg, *sang cham*. Step forward, right leg *tat*. Immediately *sang kai*. Step back with right foot, face the right, the rear, the left and then the front with *sang kwi kieng*. Step back overlapping to face front, *kwi kieng*. Turn to the front, *sang tsuan*. Turn to face rear, *sang tsuan*. Step forward with left leg, left hand *kai*. Right hand *chiat*. Overlapping step, then rotate to face front, right hand *kai*. Left hand *chiat*. Step back with right leg, *che bi chiu*. Step forward to the left corner, *kap*. *Chiat*. Step forward to the right corner, *kap*. *Chiat*. Step back, left hand *kai*. Step forward with right leg, *sang pueh*. Double step back, *sang puah*. Conclude by standing erect.

雙劍第五節 - DOUBLE STRAIGHT SWORDS – 5TH SECTION

踏右足戴。踏左足雙斬。踏右足雙批。向左畔左手開。踏右足右手破。退馬屈。右手斬。踏右足右手開。左手切。向後方左手開。踏右足雙批。向右畔左手開。踏右足右手破。退馬屈右手斬。踏右足右手開。左手切。向前左手開。踏右足雙批。旋螺跳向前雙破。收立正。

Step forward with right leg, *ti*. Step forward with left leg, *sang cham*. Step forward with right leg, *sang pueh*. Face the left side, left hand *kai*. Step forward with right leg, right hand *puah*. Step back into a crouch, right hand *cham*. Step forward with right leg, right hand *kai*. Left hand *chiat*. Face the rear, left hand *kai*. Step forward with right leg, *sang pueh*. Face the right side, left hand *kai*. Step forward with right leg, right hand *puah*. Step back into a crouch, right hand *cham*. Step forward with right leg, right hand *kai*, left hand *chiat*. Face the front, left hand *kai*. Step forward with right leg, *sang pueh*. Whirlwind jump facing front, *sang puah*. Conclude by standing erect.

雙劍第六節 - DOUBLE STRAIGHT SWORDS – 6TH SECTION

踏右足戴。踏左足雙斬。踏右足雙批。疊退雙破。疊進右手箭。疊退右手箭。
走馬向右屈押。切。向左屈押。切。踏右足雙批。旋螺跳向前雙破。跳向後雙
批。榻轉向左畔雙批。榻轉向右畔雙批。向後方開切。翻前右足蹀。並雙開。
疊退雙破。立正。

Step forward with right leg, *ti*. Step forward with left leg, *sang cham*. Step forward with right leg, *sang pueh*. Double step backward, *sang puah*. Double step forward, right hand *tsi*. Double step backward, right hand *tsi*. Walking step to face the right side in a crouch, *kap*. *Chiat*. Face the left in a crouch, *kap*. *Chiat*. Step forward with right leg, *sang pueh*. Whirlwind jump facing front, *sang puah*. Jump to face the rear, *sang pueh*. Overlapping step, then rotate to face the left side, *sang pueh*. Overlapping step, then rotate to face the right side, *sang pueh*. Face the rear, *kai, chiat*. Turn to the front, right leg *tat*. Immediately *sang kai*. Double step backward, *sang puah*. Stand erect.

雙劍第七節 - DOUBLE STRAIGHT SWORDS – 7TH SECTION

踏右足戴。踏左足雙斬。踏右足雙批。疊退雙破。走馬向右角雙批。走馬向左
角雙批。退左足右手開。退右足左手開。踏右足右手破。退馬屈。右手斬。進
屈右角押。切。進屈左角押。切。踏右足雙批。旋螺跳向前雙破。閃榻右畔向
前雙開弓。閃榻左畔向前雙開弓。換左足雙撟中。換右足雙破。收立正。

Step forward with right leg, *ti*. Step forward with left leg, *sang cham*. Step forward with right leg, *sang pueh*. Double step backward, *sang puah*. Walking step to face the right corner, *sang pueh*. Walking step to face the left corner, *sang pueh*. Step back with left leg, right hand *kai*. Step back with right leg, left hand *kai*. Step forward with right leg, right hand *puah*. Step back into a crouch, right hand *cham*. Step forward to the right corner in a crouch, *kap*. *Chiat*. Step forward to the left corner in a crouch, *kap*. *Chiat*. Step forward with right leg, *sang pueh*. Whirlwind jump facing the front, *sang puah*. Evade with an overlapping step to the right side, still facing front, *sang kwi kieng*. Evade overlapping to the left side, still facing front, *sang kwi kieng*. Shift to the left leg, *sang kiao* to the center. Shift to the right leg, *sang puah*. Conclude by standing erect.

雙劍第八節 – DOUBLE STRAIGHT SWORDS – 8TH SECTION

踏右足戴。踏左足雙斬。踏右足右手開。左手切。榻轉向後左手開。右手切。
退榻向後方雙開弓。翻向後雙轉。翻向前雙轉。踏左足左手開。右手切。閃左
畔齊眉手。閃右畔齊眉手。進左角押。切。進右角押。切。退右足左手開。踏
右足右手破。退馬屈右手斬。踏右足雙批。疊退雙破。收立正。

Step forward with right leg, *ti*. Step forward with left leg, *sang cham*. Step forward with right leg, *kai*. Left hand *chiat*. Overlapping step, then rotate to face rear, left hand *kai*. Right hand *chiat*. Step back overlapping to face the rear, *sang kwi kieng*. Turn to face the rear, *sang tsuan*. Turn to face the front, *sang tsuan*. Step forward with left leg, left hand *kai*, right hand *chiat*. Evade to the left side, *che bi chiu*. Evade to the right side, *che bi chiu*. Step forward to the left corner, *kap*. *Chiat*. Step forward to the right corner, *kap*. *Chiat*. Step back with the right leg, right hand *cham*. Step forward with right leg, right hand *puah*. Step back into a crouch, right hand *cham*. Step forward with right leg, *sang pueh*. Double step backward, *sang puah*. Conclude by standing erect.

雙劍練習法
DOUBLE STRAIGHT SWORD PRACTICE METHOD

即蛟龍戲水
"RIVER DRAGON PLAYS IN THE WATER"

榻進請。退寄請。退右足雙斬。踏右足雙斬。踏左足左手開。退左足右手開。向左畔雙轉。翻右畔雙轉。向前左手開。踏右足右手破。直進雙批。疊退雙截。疊進批。旋螺跳向前雙破。疊進右手開。左手切。退右足齊眉手。進左角押。切。進右角押。切。退右足左手開。踏右足右手破。退馬屈。右手斬。踏右足戴。並刈。右手挑。左手切。榻馬雙開弓。翻前雙轉。翻後雙轉。踏左足左手開。右手切。榻轉向前右手開。左手切。閃榻右畔向前雙開。閃榻左畔向前雙開。退向左畔開。換右足開。翻右畔左手開。換右足開。向前左手開。踏右足箭。退左手箭。退右手箭。榻轉向左畔雙押。榻轉向右畔雙押。榻轉向前雙批。換右足雙批。疊退雙破。收立正。

Do an overlapping step forward and perform the salutation. Step back to a hanging leg stance and perform the salutation. Step back with right leg, *sang cham*. Step forward with right leg, *sang cham*. Step forward with left leg, left hand *kai*. Step back with left leg, right hand *kai*. Face the left side, *sang tsuan*. Turn to the right side, *sang tsuan*. Face the front, left hand *kai*. Step forward with right leg, right hand *puah*. Step straight forward, *sang pueh*. Double step back, *sang chà*. Double step forward, *sang pueh*. Whirlwind jump facing front, *sang puah*. Double step forward, right hand *kai*. Left hand *chiat*. Step back with right leg, *che bi chiu*. Step forward to the left corner, *kap*. *Chiat*. Step forward to the right corner, *kap*. *Chiat*. Step back with right leg, left hand *kai*. Step forward with right leg, righ hand *puah*. Step back into a crouch, right hand *cham*. Step forward with right leg, *ti*. Immediately *kua*. Right hand *tioh,* left hand *chiat*. Overlapping step, *kwi kieng*. Turn to the front, *sang tsuan*. Turn to the rear, *sang tsuan*. Step forward with left leg, left hand *kai,* right hand *chiat*. Overlapping step, then rotate to face front, right hand *kai,* left hand *chiat*. Evade overlapping to the right side, still facing front, *sang kai*. Evade with an overlapping step to the left side, still facing front, *sang kai*. Step back to face the left side, *kai*. Shift to right leg, *kai*. Turn to face the right side, left hand *kai*. Shift to right leg, *kai*. Face the front, left hand *kai*. Step forward with right leg, *tsi*. Step back left hand *tsi*. Step back, right hand tsi. Overlapping step, then rotate to face the left side, *sang kap*. Overlapping step, then rotate to face the right side, *sang kap*. Overlapping step, then rotate to face front, *sang pueh*. Shift to right leg, *sang pueh*. Double step backward, *sang puah*. Conclude by standing erect.

25

Alex Co poses with sang tsuan pian

Russ Smith poses with sang tsuan pian

Mark Anthony Novero poses with sang tsuan pian

Bonie Lim poses with sang tsuan pian

彩鳳雙飛 - ELEGANT DOUBLE FLYING PHOENIX

搨進請。退寄請。退右足雙拳。平右手斬。搨馬開。平馬左手斬。搨馬開。換右足擒。撞。換左足擒。撞。退右手擒。退左手刈。退雙轉。疊進雙批。退夾屈。呈身左手擒。踏右足刈。閃馬開。右手摔。退雙破。翻後右足躂。並開。換左足擒。撞。換右足擒。撞。退左手擒。退右手刈。退雙轉。疊進雙批。退夾屈。呈身右手擒。踏左足刈。閃馬開。左手摔。退雙破。翻前左足躂。並開。踏右足雙橋。搨向左畔開。切。搨向右畔開。切。向前左手開。踏右足破。退馬屈。右手斬。踏右足戴。並刈。右挑。左切。搨馬開弓。翻前雙轉。翻後雙轉。踏左足雙批。搨馬向前雙批。旋螺跳向前雙破。搨進請。退寄請。退夾雙拳。收立正。曲手。垂下。

Step forward overlapping and perform the salutation. Step back to a hanging leg stance and perform the salutation. Step back with right leg, *sang kun*. Assume an even stance, right hand *cham*. Overlapping step, *kai*. Assume an even stance, left hand *cham*. Overlapping step, *kai*. Shift to the right leg, *kim*. *Chieng*. Shift to the left leg, *kim*. *Chieng*. Step back, right hand *kim*. Step back, left hand *kua*. Step back, *sang tsuan*. Double step forward, *sang pueh*. Step back, tuck and crouch. Rise up, left hand *kim*. Step forward with right leg, *kua*. Evade, *kai*. Right hand *sut*. Step back, *sang puah*. Turn to the rear, right leg *tat*. Immediately *kai*. Shift to the left leg, *kim*. *Chieng*. Shift to the right leg, *kim*. *Chieng*. Step back, left hand *kim*. Step back, right hand *kua*. Step back, *sang tsuan*. Double step forward, *sang pueh*. Step back, tuck and crouch. Rise up, right hand *kim*. Step forward with left leg, *kua*. Evade, kai. Left hand sut. Step back, *sang puah*. Turn to the front, left leg *tat*. Immediately *kai*. Step forward with right leg, *sang kiao*. Overlapping step to face the left side, *kai*. *Chiat*. Overlapping step to face the right side, *kai*. *Chiat*. Face the front, left hand *kai*. Step forward with right leg, *puah*. Step back into a crouch. Right hand *cham*. Step forward with right leg, *ti*. Immediately *kua*. Right hand *tioh*, left hand *chiat*. Overlapping step, *kwi kieng*. Turn to the front, *sang tsuan*. Turn to the rear, *sang tsuan*. Step forward with left leg, *sang pueh*. Overlapping step to face front, *sang pueh*. Whirlwind jump facing front, *sang puah*. Do an overlapping step forward and perform the salutation. Step back to a hanging leg stance and perform the salutation. Step back with right leg, *sang kiap kun*. Conclude by standing erect. Bend the arms and drop them downward.

26

梅花鎗 - **Mui Hue Chiu**
PLUM FLOWER SPEAR

Mark Wiley posing with spear

Alfredo Yu posing with spear

Willy Key posing with spear

三六法
THIRTY-SIX METHODS

萬里風雲
"TEN THOUSAND MILES OF STORMS"

進點左。點右。進截。過挑右。過橋左。平馬掃。平馬橋。踏右足掃。並破。
退向後過攔。榻轉向前斬。榻轉向右押上。榻轉向左斬上。疊進中過攔。旋螺
跳向前破。跳向後過攔。踏左足斬。踏右足反斬。進橋中。退向前過攔。踏左
角斬。踏右角戴。踏左角戴。踏右足戴中。閃榻押下。閃榻截左。平馬過攔。
轉斬左。走馬屈押右。轉斬左。退寄押下。平馬斬。踏右足過攔。疊退截。
捲。箭。收截立正。

Step forward, *tiam* to the left. *Tiam* to the right. Step forward, *chà*. *Ke, tioh* to the right. *Ke, kiao* to the left. Assume an even stance, *sao*. Still in an even stance, *kiao*. Step forward with right leg, *sao*. Immediately *puah*. Step back to face the rear, *ge*. Overlapping step, then rotate to face front, *cham*. Overlapping step, then rotate to the right side, *kap* upward. Overlapping step, then rotate to the left side, *cham* upward. Double step forward to the center, *ge*. Whirlwind jump facing front, *puah*. Jump to face rear, *ge*. Step forward with the left leg, *cham*. Step forward with the right leg, reverse *cham*. Step forward, *kiao* to the center. Step back to face front, *ge*. Step to the left corner, *cham*. Step to the right corner, *ti*. Step to the left corner, *ti*. Step forward with right leg, *ti* to the center. Evade with an overlapping step, *kap* downward. Evade with an overlapping step, *chà* to the left. Assume an even stance, *ge*. *Tsuan cham* to the left. Walking step, then crouch, *kap* to the right. *Tsuan cham* to the left. Step back to a hanging leg stance, *kap* downward. Assume an even stance, *cham*. Step forward with right leg, *ge*. Double step backward, *chà*. *K'n. Tsi.* Conclude with *chà*, then stand erect.

27 方天戟 - Hong Pian Kiat
SKY HALBERD

三六法
THIRTY SIX METHODS

野外風坡
WILD OUTSIDE WIND HILL

踏右足搭。平馬橋。退寄押。平馬斬。踏右足挑。退寄扭。並箭。
跳退平馬橋。踏右足挑。退寄截。走馬挑右。走馬橋左。退寄押。
平馬斬。踏右足過攔。旋螺跳向前破。平馬屈押右。屈斬左。進中
屈押上。呈身閃截。抽進插。退向後過攔。平馬斬。走馬押右。
走馬斬左。退寄押。平馬斬。踏右足過攔。榻轉向前斬。退榻橫馬
押。走馬插。退寄押。並扭。點。掇。箭。收截立正。

Step forward with right leg, *ta*. Assume an even stance, *kiao*. Step back to
a hanging leg stance, *kap*. Assume an even stance, *cham*. Step forward with
right leg, *tioh*. Step back to a hanging leg stance, *liu*. Immediately, *tsi*.
Jump back to an even stance, *kiao*. Step forward with right leg, *tioh*. Step back to a
hanging leg stance, *chà*. Walking step, *tioh* to the right. Walking step, *kiao* to
the left. Step back to a hanging leg stance, *kap*. Assume an even stance, *cham*.
Step forward with right leg, *ge*. Whirlwind jump facing front, *puah*. Assume
an even stance, then crouch and *kap* to the right. Walking step, *cham* to the
left. Step back to a hanging leg stance, *kap*. Assume an even stanceh, *cham*.
Step forward with right leg, *ge*. Overlapping step, then rotate to face front,
cham. Overlapping step back to a horizontal stance, *kap*. Walking step, *cha*.
Step back to a hanging leg stance, *kap*. Immediately liu. *Tiam. Kwa. Tsi.* Conclude with *chà,* then stand erect.

Appendix:
Beng Kiam Athletic Association

Editor's Note: *This Appendix was not part of the original book.*

THE PHILIPPINE-CHINESE BENG KIAM ATHLETIC ASSOCIATION

Ngo Cho Kun was created by Chua Giok Beng (1853–1903) during the declining years of the Ching dynasty (1644–1911). Chua combined the best of the existing five famous styles of kung-fu from Fukien at that time into a composite style. It was therefore made up of the following styles: peho (white crane), Tai Cho (Sung dynasty emperor boxing), lohan (Buddhist arhat methods), kao kun (monkey), and tat chun (Bodhidharma's method). Chua called his style ngo cho kun, or "fist of the five ancestors," in honor of the five styles he combined and classified his style techniques into finger strike of the white crane, palm technique from the monkey, kicking technique from emperor boxing, footwork from lohan boxing and the body postures of Tamo.

As Chua's reputation grew, he accepted many disciples. The more famous ones are known as the "Ngo Cho Ten Tigers." Among them is Tan Kiong Beng, a wealthy merchant who travelled to the Philippines in the early 1900s, where he made his living as a bone setter. Tan's expertise in Ngo Cho Kun was soon discovered by the overseas Chinese in Manila, who persuaded him to teach Ngo Cho Kun. Tan accepted a few disciples. In 1935, Tan's students in Manila requested him to formally open a school in the Philippines.

Tan wanted to enjoy his twilight years in his hometown in Fukien, China, so he sent his son, Tan Ka Hong, to Manila in his place. Equipped with only a few kung-fu weapons and a sworn promise to spread the art, Tan Ka Hong set sail for the Philippines. There he established the Beng Kiam Club in 1935 with the help of some of his father's disciples. This school was to become the pioneer kung-fu school in Manila. Ngo Cho Kun has since spread from Manila to different parts of the Philippines and America through the students of Tan Ka Hong.

Today the Beng Kiam Athletic Association is run by Tan's son, Benito Tan, and his classmates Alex Co, Willy Keh, Daniel Go, Alfredo Ngo, Tony Lim, Jose Ang, and William Uy. In the United States Beng Kiam is being represented by Bonifacio Lim, Ben Asuncion, Mark Wiley, Kiko Capinpin, and students of the late Christopher Rickets.

In 1998, Beng Kiam presented Mark Wiley with an official banner authorizing him to open The American Beng Hong Athletic Association to propagate Ngo Cho Kun in the West. Headquartered in Metro Philadelphia, PA the Association is open to all and has official members throughout the United States, Canada and Europe, including Russ Smith in Florida, Keith Boggess in Pennsylvania and Simon T. Lailey in the United Kingdom.

Tan Kiong Beng

Tan Ka Hong

Alex Co & Ang Hua Kun

Tony Lim & William Tan, 1980s

Benito Tan, Tan Ka Hong, Hua Kun

Alex Co & Leonardo Co, 71st Anniversary Demo

Beng Kiam students in late 1960s

In the past, Beng Kiam was an exclusive association, open only by invitation from members of the club. In 2010 Beng Kiam opened its doors to everyone, regardless of ethnicity and social class. And in 2013 Sifu Alex Co opened an official branch in Makati City, Philippines for those interested in studying who are unable to make it to the Binondo headquarters.

At Beng Kiam, students can expect to learn one of the best traditional southern Chinese martial arts. As a whole, Ngo Cho Kun is a comprehensive and complete system of Chinese martial arts. It covers skills in hand techniques, leg techniques, escaping, locking, throwing and even ground fighting. One of its unique aspects is the development of the iron body, a skill that allows one to withstand blows with little ill effect. Practitioners of Ngo Cho Kun become strong without distorting or disfiguring their bodies. This is done through the use of natural movements blended into patterns that enable the practitioner's strength and power to increase noticeably. While Ngo Cho Kun is primarily a martial art, its practitioners are noticeably healthy and robust, even up to the senior years. Regular practice has been known to help regulate one's blood pressure, a fact of interest to many. In addition, the lively and dynamic movements of the style help improve the overall fitness of the practitioner. Thus, it has something for everyone, from effective self-defense to health and long life.

At The Beng Kiam Athletic Club, Binondo, Manila, Philippines. Standing (L to R): Ernie Go, George Kwan, George Go, Willy Keh, Jimmy So, Juan Tiu, William Uy, Jose Ang, Mark Anthony Novero.   Seated (L to R): Leonardo Co, Benito Tan, Alfredo Yu, Alex Co.

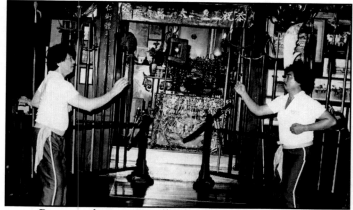

Partners throwing 20 lb *chio-so*, iron-lock weight.

William Uy

William Tan presenting souviner books to Chen Tai Chi master Feng Tzi Chiang during Beijing trip in 1991. With Alex Co, Anfonzo Ang Hua Kun, Vincent Go.

Benito Tan magazine cover, 1978

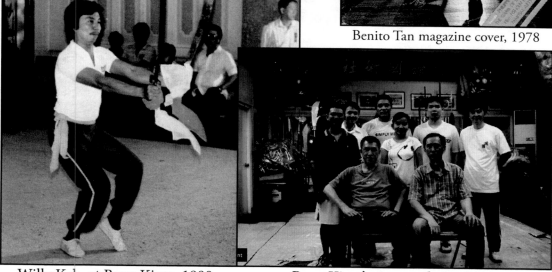

Willy Keh, at Beng Kiam, 1980s

Beng Kiam's new students, 2010

Mark Wiley testing Ang Hua Kun's "iron throat"

Alex Co & Christopher Ricketts

Alex Co showing *fa-jing* power

Members of Beng Kiam in 1990s, Benito Tan sits center

Bonifacio Lim & Alex Co

Paying respects at the grave of Tan Kiong Beng, 1991

Bonifacio Lim

Willey Key demonstrating the horse-cutter

Opening of Beng Kiam Makati Branch, 2013
with Alex Co, Ronnie Ricketts, Benito Tan

Russ Smith, Alex Co, Aldredo Yu, Mark Wiley at
Beng Kiam Athletic Club, 2013

Jimmy So demonstrating tri-sectional pole

Tondy Diego, Topher Ricketts, Rey Galang, Ang
Hua Kun, Mark Wiley, Alex Co, 1994

Russ Smith with Alex Co, in Sifu Co's home in Makati, Philippines, working on this book, 2013

Peter Schofield

Simon T. Lailey

Alex Co & Mark Wiley, 2013

Keith Boggess

Kiko Capinpin tossing *chio-so* weight

Christopher Ricketts, Alexander Lim Co, Bonifacio Lim, Mark Wiley, 1998

ABOUT THE TRANSLATORS & EDITOR

ALEXANDER LIM CO is a living treasure in the arts of Chinese kung-fu. In fact, no name is more synonymous with Kung-Fu in the Philippines than his. Co spearheaded the Chin Wu Club in Manila, wrote the first kung-fu book ever published in the Philippines, and published the country's first martial arts magazine, simply titled *Martial Arts Magazine*. Grandmaster Co has studied a dozen different kung-fu styles, was an "in-door" disciple of Ngo Cho Kun's late grandmaster Tan Ka Hong, and has studied Seven Star Praying Mantis and Hung-gar under Sifu Shakespeare Chan, Wu style Tai Chi Chuan under the late Sifu Hu Chuan Hai, and Hsin-I Liu Ha Pa Fa under the late Sifu David Chan. Alex Co has served as Chairman of the Philippine-Chinese Beng Kiam Athletic Association and the Tsing Hua Ngo Cho Kung-fu Center and as Vice-chairman of the Hsin-I Society of Internal Arts. In addition to dozens of articles, Sifu Co has written three books: *Secrets of Seven Star Praying Mantis*, *The Way of Ngo Cho Kun* and *Five Ancestor Fist Kung-Fu*. He also filmed a series of instructional videos *The Essence of Ngo Cho Kun* and *Secrets of Seven Star Mantis* for Unique Publications Video.

RUSS L. SMITH expressed an interest in martial arts as a teenager and began Karate basics with a family friend. It wasn't until Russ was on extended vacation in the Philippines over twenty-five years ago that he began formal training in Japanese Goju-Ryu under an Sensei Iyan Mackenzie. Upon his return to the USA, Russ's interest in the origins of Goju-Ryu were piqued and led to him seeking out instruction in Okinawan Goju-Ryu. Smith's desire to continue research on the origins and influences on Goju-Ryu has lead him to also study Fujian and Hakka arts such as Ngo Cho Kun, Pak Mei and White Crane Boxing. Russ makes periodic trips overseas to train Goju-Ryu and Kobudo in Okinawa, and Kung Fu in Malaysia, Singapore, the Phillippines, and across the USA. His focus is preserving, promoting, and researching the arts of Okinawa, Southern China, Malaysia, and the Philippines at his Burinkan dojo.

DR. MARK V. WILEY is President of the American Beng Hong Athletic Association. A disciple of Sifu Alexander Lim Co, Dr. Wiley began his martial arts training 34 years ago. Since his first day on the path he has been deeply involved in all aspects of the arts, from training and teaching to researching, writing and publishing. He is passionate about the history and culture of Chinese and Filipino martial arts. Since 1994, Dr. Wiley has been conducting extensive training and research on location in the Philippines, Malaysia, Singapore, Taiwan and Japan. During that time he lived in Tokyo and made an impressive 15 visits to the Philippines. He holds a Masters Degree in Health Care Management and Doctorates in both Oriental Medicine and Alternative Medicine, wherein his understanding of the human mind, body and energy systems has deepened his understanding and application of the martial arts. Dr. Wiley has authored 15 books and over 500 articles.

CONTACT INFORMATION

BENG KIAM BRANCHES

Grandmaster Benito Tan
Binondo, Manila, Philippines
Local Phone: (632) 4589215
www.BengKiam.com

Sifu Alexander Lim Co
Makati City, Philippines
Local Phone: (632) 4589215
ngochokun612@yahoo.com

Sifu Bonifacio Lim
Plainsboro, New Jersey
bonifaciolim@yahoo.com

Sifu Kiko Capinpin
Baltimore, Maryland
xcap19@yahoo.com

BENG HONG BRANCHES

Dr. Mark V. Wiley
Lansdale, Pennsylvania
mvwiley@gmail.com
www.NgoChoKun.Wordpress.com

Sifu Russ L. Smith
Zephyrhills, Florida
Russ.L.Smith@gmail.com
www.Burinkan.org

Sifu Keith Boggess
West Chester, Pennsylvania
Keith@BoggessLawOffice.com

Sifu Simon T. Lailey
Isle of Wight, England
realkungfu@talktalk.net

Tambuli Media

Excellence in Mind-Body Health & Martial Arts Publishing

Welcome to Tambuli Media, publisher of quality books on mind-body health and martial arts presented in their cultural context.

Our Vision is to see quality books once again playing an integral role in the lives of people who pursue a journey of personal development, through the documentation and transmission of traditional knowledge of mind-body cultures.

Our Mission is to partner with the highest caliber subject-matter experts to bring you the highest quality books on important topics of health and martial arts that are in-depth, well-written, clearly illustrated and comprehensive.

Tambuli is the name of a native instrument in the Philippines fashioned from the horn of a carabao. The tambuli was blown and its sound signaled to villagers that a meeting with village elders was to be in session, or to announce the news of the day. It is hoped that Tambuli Media publications will "bring people together and disseminate the knowledge" to many.

  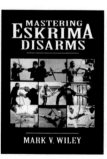  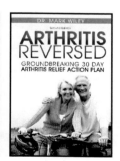

www.TambuliMedia.com

Made in United States
North Haven, CT
23 August 2024

56471029R00135